Margaret Doyle was born in California, USA, in 1963 and grew up in St Louis. She graduated from Barnard College in New York with a degree in women's studies, and lived and worked in New York City for nine years before moving to Britain in 1990. She is a freelance writer and editor and lives with her husband and one-year-old daughter in West London, where she is also a volunteer community mediator for neighbour disputes.

MARGARET DOYLE

the
A–Z
of
Non-Sexist
Language

First published by The Women's Press Ltd, 1995
A member of the Namara Group
34 Great Sutton Street, London EC1V 0DX

British Library Cataloguing-in-Publication Data
A catalogue record for this book is available from the British
Library

ISBN 0 7043 4430 0

Phototypeset in Sabon 10/12pt by Intype, London
Printed and bound in Great Britain by
BPC Paperbacks Ltd, Aylesbury, Bucks

For Oliver and Anneliese, finders of new words

Acknowledgements

I am grateful to the representatives of all the organisations mentioned in the book for giving their time, discussing their organisations' policies with me, and sending written guidelines and other materials. I am also grateful to all at The Women's Press for their support: Kathy Gale and Helen Windrath; and Maggy Hendry for insightful copy-editing.

Many thanks are due to those friends and family who read and commented on the introduction and offered suggestions from many perspectives: Jane Robertson and Louise Clairmonte, my parents Dorothy Doyle and James Doyle, and especially my sister Helen Doyle, one of the sharpest, most thoughtful readers I know.

To the book's silent co-author, Oliver Marshall, I owe thanks in abundance – not only for keeping my enthusiasm for the project from waning, but for tempering doubts along the way and, most of all, keeping an eye and ear tuned at all times for usages with which to expand my word list.

Contents

Contents

Introduction

The English language has far more lives than a cat. People have been murdering it for years.

Farmers' Almanac

English can credit its survival to its marvellous adaptability. New words make their way quite easily into common usage, while words that fall out of favour are gently shed, giving the language a fluidity that allows it to respond to changes in society. On the other hand, we can be stubborn language users, clinging to archaic rules and usages as if they were inscribed in stone. Yet there are problems with English usage when it does not reflect the way we live. It becomes awkward, ambiguous, inaccurate, and insensitive. If our language leads to misunderstandings or offends people we are trying to reach, it fails to do what we want it to do; it ceases to be an effective tool for communication. Language that is sexist has this effect.

What is sexist language?

'Sexist language' in this book refers to terms and usages that exclude or discriminate against women. This includes presuming that maleness is standard, the norm, and that femaleness is non-standard, or the exception. One way this most often manifests itself is in the use of 'he/his/him' pronouns and terms like 'man' and 'mankind' to represent women as well as men. Another way is in the use of job titles ending in ' –man'. These are often considered to be 'generic' terms, when people using them believe they are genderless, representing neither male nor female subjects, or that they are inclusive, representing both male and female subjects. 'Businessman' (especially in its plural form), 'salesman' and 'chairman' are commonly used in this way.

Another term for sexist language is 'exclusive' language:

using *he* as a generic pronoun, and using *mankind* and ' –man' compounds as generic terms, excludes women. We associate these with maleness; they bring male images to mind. The opposite, non-sexist language, is thus also known as 'inclusive' language. There are many other types of inclusive language; truly inclusive language would attempt to include all groups that are marginalised by the presumption of a norm that is white, male, heterosexual, middle class. This book, however, deals only with non-sexist inclusive language.

Language is sexist, and exclusive, in many other ways. It can be used to promote sexist stereotypes of, for example, men's and women's roles in society or male and female characteristics. Referring to 'mother and toddler playgroups' or 'mothers' helpers', for example, suggests that men take a secondary role in looking after children and household chores. While it might be true that many do, some do not; and by perpetuating this stereotype, this language may give support to the idea that this division of roles is acceptable. It may also make it easier for some men to justify not taking on this role and harder for others to feel comfortable doing so. Referring to a fussy person (usually a man) as 'an old woman' suggests that older women are, as a rule, fussy and complaining. Though some certainly might be, so are some older men, and younger men, and younger women. Older women are no more likely to be fussy or complaining than are members of any of these other groups – yet the inaccurate stereotype persists in this phrase.

Using inclusive language does not have to be clumsy. Nor does it necessarily remove the 'colour' from our language. Most sexist terms have many alternatives, and replacing them can be easy. The result will be clearer, more accurate, and more widely received language.

Why be concerned?

The reason for avoiding sexist language is that it can be used to discriminate against women not only by reinforcing harmful stereotypes but also by rendering women's presence and achievements invisible. Many people believe that discrimination in society will not change simply by ridding our language of sexism. In this view, using non-sexist language is only paying lip-service to reform rather than addressing the very real problems of sexism in society, including discrimination, harassment, violence against women, and economic inequality. Furthermore, in this view, efforts to adopt non-sexist language can be harmful because they can provide a superficially progressive veneer for an organisation while masking its systemic sexism. Others believe that using non-sexist language is an essential part of tackling societal sexism. In this view, language influences our attitudes and behaviour; watching our language goes hand in hand with being careful how we treat others.

Ultimately, the question many people ask is 'why change?' There are as many reasons as there are ways: because sexist language is unclear and inaccurate, because it excludes more than half the population, because it encourages destructive stereotypes, because it hurts. It is also bad for business, and it makes clear communication difficult. We do ourselves a disservice when we use sexist language when writing or speaking because it is often ambiguous. When a pollster goes out to investigate what 'the man on the street' thinks of the prime minister, is she or he also investigating the views of 'the woman on the street'? This is an important distinction; the two will most likely have quite different opinions. Effective communication also requires reaching out to your target audience. Because many people are offended by sexist language, by using it you run the risk of losing the attention of those you intend to reach.

The aims of this book are to put a spotlight on the sexism in our language and bring it to people's attention, and to make it easier to use non-sexist language wherever possible. It is also intended to encourage the creation of organisational guidelines specifically addressing sexist language and making practical recommendations for change. Many professional bodies have established such guidelines for their members and/or employees, and these are described here as examples of the positive changes taking place in Britain today. In highlighting these individual efforts, I am not suggesting that this is all that needs to be done. Clearly, using inclusive or gender-specific terms (rather than male-based terms used as generics) for job titles, for example, will not obliterate job or pay discrimination against women. But using inclusive terms and, where appropriate, using both male and female terms (*spokesman* and *spokeswoman*, for example) helps to make women more visible, both to the public and within organisations; it sends a signal that women's presence (or lack of it) must be addressed. For an organisation to be effective in recruiting female staff, attracting female customers, and serving the needs of a public that is at least half female, it must make positive efforts to reach out to women and to reflect their concerns and accomplishments. Using language that puts women on an equal basis with men is one (albeit not the only, but often the most visible) method of doing this.

Political correctness

Language is often identified as a key issue in the debate about political correctness, or PC as it is known. The origins of the term continue to be debated – some claim it started out as a label created by the right wing for a movement on American campuses to expand the traditional curriculum; others that it is a term coined by the left as a self-deprecating description of some of its own party-line attitudes. Today, the label has become a broad brush applied to any effort to reflect our changing society that goes against the status quo. That is why it is most often characterised as a tool employed by the left and, in the 'backlash' against feminism, by women in particular, who, conservatives feel, mutilate language in the name of ideology.

The struggle for control of language has always been a political and highly charged one, however. (Consider, for example, the Conservative Government's appropriation of the language of the liberal left, where 'care in the community' and 'empowerment' now mean cuts in welfare and service provision.) For generations our use of language has adapted to reflect changes in society and sensibilities, most recently as the hard-won result of social struggle against discrimination. Replacing 'crippled' with 'disabled' or 'Negro' with 'black' are not new efforts, nor are they resisted – these days – by most members of society. They had to be fought for, however, and are part of broader movements (in themselves much older than the term 'PC'), one aim of which has been to give members of marginalised groups the opportunity to define how they would like to be described by others. (One aspect of this move is the 'reclaiming' of negative terms. Some terms that are considered offensive as 'labels' are being adopted among members of the labelled group as positive, self-defining terms. 'Nigger' and 'queer' are two examples.) Like efforts to combat sexism in language, these fights for self-identity have long, distinguished histories tied to struggles for self-determination and equality. They are some of the many constant shifts we make in our use of language.

'Political correctness' has attracted a great deal of media and press attention and has become a useful (though wildly misapplied) label for ridiculing an opposing viewpoint. The most common examples cited of the absurdity of PC language – 'vertically challenged' for 'short', and other such ' –challenged' compounds – are products of imagination. No one uses or proposes to use such terms. They are, however, one aspect of the way that inclusive language is confused with euphemism. But the effect of such caricatures is to attempt to discredit the legitimate aspirations of different communities and their desire for a language that includes rather than excludes them, and to undermine the important gains that have been made in achieving general acceptance of non-sexist language and effecting positive change. Inclusive language is not narrow and prescriptive; it does not aim to create a canon of 'politically correct' words. It aims instead to clarify and distinguish, to move away from labelling and name-calling. In so doing, it reflects the positive changes taking place in our society; it enables, and genuinely empowers.

Which words or usages are sexist?

Everyone has her or his own definition of what constitutes sexist language. What is sexist to one person may be acceptable usage to another. Many people, for instance, look to the origins of a word – its etymology – to investigate its original meaning and determine if it is sexist. Words like *patron* and *patronising* derive from the Latin for 'father'; *dominate* derives from the Latin for 'lord'. Because of this, some people may object to their use as generic terms applied to women and men. Analysing a word's derivation is not always helpful, however, as its original meaning may be far removed from its current use – *patron* and *patronising* are used equally for women and men today. Other words, like *fellow*, are not sexist in their origin but through the years have acquired masculine meaning ('that fellow over there' can only be a man; '(she's/he's) a jolly good fellow', however, can be either). *Master* is used sometimes as a generic (*taskmaster*, *masterpiece*) and sometimes as a sex-specific term (*schoolmaster*). Most people rely on the context and the way the word is used when deciding whether the word is objectionable; referring to all who manage local post offices as 'postmasters' may be sexist, whereas calling an original a 'master copy' may not be. Some people, however, prefer to replace words incorporating 'fellow' and 'master', so alternatives are provided in the A–Z listing of the book.

Another aspect of sexist language that is referred to in this book is non-parallel treatment of female and male subjects. The terms 'Essex man' and 'Essex girl' are an example of this – calling women 'girls' and men 'men'. This demeans women and gives the impression that women are taken less seriously (unless it is a term women use for themselves: *Riot grrls* and *out with the girls* are two examples). Another type of non-parallel usage involves the connotations of the terms: the feminine term is often negative or derogatory, whereas the masculine term is often positive or at least non-judgemental (contrast, for example, *ladies' man* and *man-eater*). Similarly, many negative terms for women have no masculine counterpart, and even when counterparts exist they are often little used. *Nympho-mania*, for example, is widely used to describe the condition of a woman who is considered sexually active and eager. The masculine 'equivalent', *satyriasis*, is rarely, if ever, heard.

Non-parallel usage also appears in the common construction of adding 'and women' after a compound word incorporating ' –men' (as in 'craftsmen and women'), a mistake made in the attempt to avoid using ' –man' as a generic term, where a subject is or might be female. The correct construction is parallel – 'craftsmen and craftswomen' or 'craftswomen and craftsmen'. Using terms ending in ' –woman' and ' –man' (*saleswoman*, *salesman*) is one way to incorporate parallel usage, but it is not necessarily the best way. It can be long-winded and awkward, and in most cases it is unnecessary to specify the sex of the subject. In the above example, *craftworkers* or *artisans* would be appropriate gender-neutral alternatives. On the other hand, in some instances it might be desirable to flag the fact that some subjects are female – especially, for instance, in male-dominated professions – to combat the assumption of maleness that is usually made.

Using the book as a guide

The intention of this book is not to obliterate words or usages from the language. Some readers will feel that not all of the words listed in the book as such are objectionable. This is to be expected; we each have a different threshold of what offends us and what does not. If a term or usage is not objectionable to you, and if you feel that it will not appear sexist to others, and especially if you feel that no suitable alternative can be found, you will probably want to use that term. Its inclusion in the book is not meant to indicate that it should be 'banned' from use. Many people, however, may feel that they want to use non-sexist language but are unsure what terms and usages might be interpreted as sexist. That is why the A–Z listing is so comprehensive.

Finding your way around

This is meant to be a practical, hands-on guide that will make it easy for writers, speakers and everyone who cares about the language they use to find a non-sexist alternative that enhances their language instead of restricting it, that clarifies rather than muddies.

The main section of the book is the A–Z listing of problematic words. Finding an alternative can be as quick as looking up the word in question in the A–Z listing. Some listings include a brief discussion of the problem; others refer to more in-depth discussions contained in topic notes within the listing section. For all words that the reader wants to remove or find a substitute for, there is at least one alternative word provided under 'Options'. The Options entries should be treated like those in a thesaurus: the alternatives given will not all be synonyms of the main entry. They will have different connotations or even quite different meanings. As with a thesaurus, choosing the best alternative requires being sensitive to the context in which it will be used. If no appropriate alternative can be found, it may be possible to restructure the sentence to avoid a sexist use or construction.

The topic notes contain discussions of specific words or specific aspects of sexist language – the pronoun problem, words with feminised endings, and salutations in letters, among others. They discuss how to resolve the most common problems that arise from sexist constructions and usages and for which replacing a single word or phrase is not enough. Other topic notes describe changes taking place within organisations that have instituted specific guidelines on using inclusive language. These have been selected as examples only and are not an exhaustive list; many other professional bodies, publishers, and employers have similar guidelines. The examples included are bodies with high public profiles that have made recent changes regarding non-sexist language, including, in many cases, the production of specific guidelines for employees and/or members. It is hoped that the examples described will encourage other groups who are considering creating non-sexist guidelines but are put off by accusations of political correctness or by uncertainties about how to go about it. Using non-sexist language should be as simple and straightforward as using correct spelling, punctuation, and grammar. It should also be tailored to particular needs, as are all good employee handbooks and how-to manuals.

Adding to it

The adaptability of English means that new words make their way into the common vocabulary with remarkable frequency and speed. Because of this, sexist terms and usages that do not appear in this volume may spring to readers' minds. It is hoped that readers will add these – by actually writing them into their copies and also by suggesting them to the author, care of the publisher, to consider in future editions.

A

abbess A parallel term with *abbot* (from the Latin *abbatissa*) and not sexist when used in a gender-specific way.

abominable snowman OPTIONS: yeti, abominable snow creature.

actress Use *actor* for women or men. This and other words with the '–ess' suffix are based on masculine root forms that are considered the norm – in this case, *actor*. As long as the standard is *actor* – eg Actors' Equity – *actress* will hold less weight, and it does, according to many female actors. See topic note on page 26.
OPTIONS: actor, performer.

ad man OPTIONS: ad executive, marketer, copywriter.

adulteress See topic note on page 26. OPTION: adulterer.

adventuress See topic note on page 26.
OPTIONS: adventurer, explorer, thrill seeker.

agony aunt The 'aunt' implies a special relationship that many believe should be preserved, but there are alternatives. Males have been referred to as *agony uncles*.
OPTIONS: advice columnist, agony aunt/agony uncle.

air hostess OPTIONS: flight attendant, cabin crew member.

airman OPTIONS: pilot, aviator, airman/airwoman, flight crew member, flier.

alderman Now obsolete as an official title.
OPTIONS: councillor, council member.

all things to all men OPTION: all things to all people.

alma mater Latin for 'mother who nourishes'.
OPTIONS: former school/college/university, graduating institution, degree-awarding institution.

alumnus The feminine term, *alumna*, came into popular use as more women began graduating from universities in the late nineteenth century, long after *alumnus*. Use these terms when the sex of the person is known – or, with the plural, the group is single sex (*alumnae* for women, *alumni* for men); otherwise, replace.
OPTION: graduate (graduates).

amazon Retain (and capitalise) when referring to the female Amazon warriors of legend. Sometimes used in a derogatory way to refer to strong, tough, or large (that is, 'unfeminine') women, and so should be used carefully; but also increasingly reclaimed by women as a positive term.

ambassadress Ambiguous because of its dual meaning; do not use it for 'wife of ambassador' or for 'female ambassador'. See also **topic note** on page 26.
OPTIONS: ambassador, diplomat, emissary, envoy, minister.

ambulanceman OPTIONS: ambulance worker/driver, paramedic.

anchorman OPTIONS: newsreader, anchor, anchor person, news anchor, news presenter.

apron strings The saying 'tied to someone's apron strings' is linked to the stereotype of the over-protective mother hovering around the kitchen wearing an apron, a common (although dated) sexist image. Avoid. OPTIONS: dependent on, coddled, indulged, protected by, dominated by, controlled by.

army wife There is no parallel masculine term; men married to military personnel are not called 'army husbands'. Replace.
OPTIONS: army spouse, dependant, spouse/family of military personnel.

Aunt Sally From a skittles-like game of the same name, the term is not necessarily sexist, except that the object of the game (which is a pub game, predominantly played by men) is to knock over a female wooden doll.

au pair Until early in 1993, the Home Office had considered an *au pair* to be 'an unmarried girl aged 17 to 27' of certain nationalities and with a certain purpose in coming to Britain (HMSO, 1990). Before the change allowing *au pairs* of either sex, men had to apply as *houseboys*, for which different rules applied. Use *au pair* for both male and female.

authoress See topic note on page 26.
OPTIONS: author, writer; or be specific with, for example, novelist, poet, biographer, essayist, columnist.

aviatrix OPTIONS: aviator, pilot.

B

babe A derogatory and/or belittling term for women – especially an attractive woman – although the word is now being reclaimed by some feminists.

baccalaureate (degree) From the Latin for 'bachelor', and so sometimes replaced. 'Feminised' degrees – including Maid of Arts (or Science), Mistress of Arts, and Sister of Arts – were awarded at some US universities in the nineteenth century (Baron, 1986). Most degrees are now referred to by abbreviations (BA, MA) and are, in any case, used in a gender-neutral way.
OPTIONS: undergraduate (degree), first (degree), BA.

bachelor The 'swinging' connotation of *bachelor* does not apply to its feminine 'counterpart', SPINSTER, and so its use has sexist implications.
OPTIONS: single man, single person, unmarried person.

backwoodsman OPTIONS: backwoodsperson, hinterlander, frontiersperson, pioneer; uncouth person, rustic; backwoodser.

bag lady One rarely hears the term *bag man* (and certainly not *bag gentleman*) used to describe a homeless person – an example of unparallel usage. *Bag lady* is sometimes used to refer to any 'messy, un-feminine' woman. The term BAGMAN commonly used has a completely different meaning.
OPTIONS: bag woman (if used equally with *bag man*), homeless woman, vagrant, street person.

bagman In Britain, this word has a quite different meaning from that of *bag man*, the rarely used male 'equivalent' of BAG LADY (although in Australia the word means 'tramp').
OPTIONS: travelling sales representative, travelling salesperson.

bar maid OPTION: bartender.

barman OPTION: bartender.

baron As a general term (meaning 'leader' or 'lord' – as in 'drug baron'), use for women and men. Otherwise, as a title of nobility use for men only.

barren The use of the term *barren* contributes to the sexist assumption that a woman who cannot or does not have children is incomplete or 'empty'. There is no similar term for men with the same connotations. Replace.

OPTIONS: infertile, sterile.

barrow boy OPTIONS: market trader, stallholder, street trader, market/street vendor.

bastard Don't use to refer to a child whose father is not known or whose parents are not married; it suggests 'illegitimacy' if a child is born outside the conventional family structure of a married mother and father. If parenthood details are necessary (which they often are not), use *child of unmarried parents* or *child of a lone parent*. See also ILLEGITIMATE.

batman OPTIONS: officer's attendant, assistant.

batsman OPTIONS: batter, batsperson.

bellboy OPTIONS: bellhop, porter, hotel worker.

best man Retain if using 'best woman' as parallel term; otherwise replace. See MAID OF HONOUR.

OPTIONS: groom's attendant, best man/best woman.

best man for the job OPTIONS: best person for the job, best candidate.

bimbo There is no male parallel (although the term originally meant 'tough guy'); *bimboy* and *toy boy* are sometimes seen as equivalents for men. Avoid, as it perpetuates a sexist stereotype.

bird A sexist term for *girl*, not in such common usage as in the past, and now sometimes used in sardonic or humorous references to 1960s' slang.

bitch (noun) One of the most common and pervasive insults, originally used for both sexes but now reserved for women and, occasionally, used within gay male culture. It is one of several derogatory terms linking women with animals – eg *chick, bird, cow, shrew* – and is so identified as an insult (and often a particularly hate-filled one) that it is rarely used in its original sense of 'female dog'. It is used by women and men, and in fact there are efforts by women to reclaim it as a positive label – *The Bitch Manifesto*, for example, is a feminist tract from 1970 whose title celebrates strong, rebellious women. Nevertheless, *bitch* is most often used to describe a woman who is considered to be malicious, complaining or spiteful, and its use reinforces negative stereotypes of women. Avoid. See also NAG, SCOLD, SHREW.

bitch (verb) Although 'to bitch' is moving toward gender-neutral usage, it is still widely associated with *bitch* as a noun, which is applied almost exclusively to women and among gay men. Replace with a less loaded term.
OPTIONS: complain, gripe, moan, grumble, lecture.

black tie event OPTIONS: formal occasion, formal-dress event.

bloke Although its origins are unknown, Thomas Sutcliffe in the *Independent* suggested that it might come from *loke*, a Romany and Hindustani word for 'man'. Writing about 'mate', Sutcliffe pointed out that like bloke, 'mate' 'is too male, too connected with the sodalities of the splash-bath and the saloon bar, to sound convincing in a woman's mouth' (*Independent*, 8 April 1993). Although this is certainly open to argument, it does appear that the use of 'bloke' can encourage 'matiness', an alliance among 'the boys', so be careful how it is used. See also MATE.

blonde This 'feminine' of *blond*, as in 'the long-legged blonde', lends itself to sexist usage and is best avoided. Use *blond* for both male and female.

bluesman OPTIONS: blues musician, blues singer.

bluestocking Derives from Blue Stocking Society, a scornful term for certain eighteenth-century literary gatherings at which informal dress was the norm. Ironically, the wearer of the 'blue stockings' (actually grey) was a man. The term reflects the suspicion with which men viewed intelligent women: as threatening, and therefore unattractive and lacking in 'femininity'. It could be losing its derogatory sense as it is reclaimed by feminists, but it is still used to mock.
OPTIONS: intellectual, scholar, person of letters.

boatman OPTIONS: boat handler, boat owner, captain, skipper, rower, gondolier.

bobby Not a sexist term. Derives from Robert Peel, Home Secretary when the Metropolitan Police was formed in the mid-nineteenth century. *Peeler* was also used, especially for the Scottish and the Irish police. Use for male or female. See also **topic note** on page 76.

Bond girl Not just a sexist term (especially in its use of 'girl' for adult women), but a sexist concept in that it labels the actor herself (ie not only the role she is playing) in terms of a possession, append-age and/or conquest of James Bond. Avoid.

boss Has very different connotations when used with regard to women and men: negative for women (as an adjective, *bossy*, or a verb, *to boss*, or to be domineering) and positive for men (usually as a noun, *the boss*, or an informal salutation), or at least powerful (as in *the bosses upstairs*). Be careful to use in a parallel way for both male and female.

bouncer Use for women and men. See DOORMAN.

bovver boy These usually are male, but not necessarily so. (The term *bovver* is from 'bother', a mild term for what they supposedly cause.)
OPTIONS: bovverer, skinhead, gang member, rowdy, thug, heavy.

boy racer These usually are male, but not always so.
OPTIONS: teenager racer, joyrider, girl racer/boy racer.

boycott Not a sexist term. Derives from Charles Cunningham Boycott, a nineteenth-century estate manager who was the victim of an ostracism campaign by the Irish Land League.

boys will be boys Often carries the implication of being resigned to, and thus excusing or ignoring, immature or irresponsible behaviour in men. Thus, use the expression carefully. When used in a gender-neutral or mixed-gender sense, replace. OPTION: kids will be kids.

bra burner An insulting and inaccurate label; as many writers have shown, such burnings were a rare occurrence. Like WOMEN'S LIBBER, it is a hostile and derogatory term for feminists.

brethren Used now almost exclusively for members of religious groups and secret societies. Keep in those contexts when specifically male (eg monasteries); otherwise avoid. Use *brothers* for plural of *brother*. See also BROTHERHOOD.
OPTIONS: family, siblings, neighbours, compatriots; or be specific with, for example, fellow (name of country or town).

bridegroom For parallel usage with *bride*, use *groom*.

bridesmaid OPTIONS: bride's attendant, wedding attendant.

brinkmanship OPTIONS: risk-taking, challenging, bluffing, bluster, confrontation.

brotherhood Retain when referring to monasteries. Do not use as a generic for 'guild' or any organised or allied group (eg 'brotherhood of man'). See also SISTERHOOD.
OPTIONS: unity, community, family, friendship, humanity, sibship; guild, union, organisation, alliance.

brotherly love OPTIONS: familial love, affection, platonic love.

brunette This 'feminine' of *brunet*, as in 'the long-legged brunette', lends itself to sexist usage and is best avoided.
OPTION: brunet (use for both male and female).

bully Use for male and female.

bully boy tactics OPTIONS: bully tactics, strongarm/heavyweight tactics, browbeating.

bushman OPTIONS: bush dweller, bush inhabitant, bushperson.

Bushman The nomadic people of the Kalahari region of southern Africa refer to themselves as *San*; terms like *Bushman*, *tribal member*, and *native* are considered offensive.

businessman OPTIONS: business executive, business type, professional, industrialist, business manager, boss, entrepreneur, businessperson, manager.

busman OPTIONS: bus driver, bus conductor.

busman's holiday OPTIONS: bus driver's holiday, working holiday.

butch Used in a derogatory way to refer to an 'unfeminine' lesbian, the word is now being reclaimed by some women as a positive label.

C

call girl See PROSTITUTE.

cameraman OPTIONS: cameraperson, camera operator, photographer.

career woman/girl There is no parallel for men. The term relies on a sexist distinction between 'real' work (ie paid and outside the home) and home-based work (such as homemaking) – a distinction that is not made in relation to men. The term is ambiguous, as it is also sometimes used to distinguish between 'professional' and 'unskilled' or low-paid employment. In both cases, the subtext is that a 'career woman' sacrifices family for job. If career is important in the context, be specific – eg accountant. Otherwise, avoid.

caveman OPTIONS: cave dweller, troglodyte.

cellarman OPTIONS: cellar worker, wine officer/stocker, cellarer.

chairman Easily replaceable with a more specific term or, if a general term is wanted, with a simple gender-neutral adaptation such as *chair*. See topic notes on pages 19 and 63.
OPTIONS: chair, convenor, moderator, chairperson, chairwoman/chairman, panel or committee head, director.

chambermaid OPTIONS: cleaner, hotel cleaner, housekeeper, personal attendant.

charlady/charwoman OPTIONS: cleaner, choresperson, charworker, char.   -

checkout girl OPTIONS: till operator, cashier, checkout person, supermarket worker.

chess Some people advocate replacing sex-specific names of chess pieces, especially as the power they wield reflects a sexist hierarchy, with king at the top, although the queen has more freedom of movement.
OPTIONS: horserider, defender (knight); deputy sovereign (queen); sovereign (king).

chessman OPTIONS: chess piece; or use specific name of piece (eg rook, knight). See also CHESS.

churchman OPTIONS: church member, parishioner, church-goer, worshipper.

Cinderella The fairytale has lent the language a simple term for something or someone (usually a woman) that is undervalued, exploited or neglected, as in 'the Cinderella of airports'. Sexist when used as a stereotype of the passive woman awaiting discovery by her 'Prince Charming'; otherwise, in non-sexist usage, it is a useful metaphor.

city fathers OPTION: city leaders.

cleaning lady OPTIONS: cleaner, household helper, office cleaner.

clergyman OPTIONS: cleric, member of the clergy, priest, vicar.

coat check girl OPTIONS: coat checker, coat clerk, cloakroom attendant.

comedienne Uses the –enne suffix which, like –ess and –ette, is used to 'feminise' otherwise standard terms. See topic note on page 26. OPTIONS: comedian, comic, entertainer, stand-up comic.

committeeman OPTION: committee member.

common man Replace with a general inclusive term, or use a term specific to the context (eg *average consumer, typical voter*). OPTIONS: ordinary person, average citizen.

compatriot Used inclusively for male and female, so in spite of being rooted in the masculine PATRIOT (from the Greek *pater*, for 'father'), it does not necessarily have sexist connotations. Some people prefer to replace it, but the options may be no less objectionable because of their reliance on FELLOW.
OPTIONS: fellow citizen; give specific nationality – eg fellow Bulgarian; comrade, neighbour.

concubine Refers only to women in a sexual relationship with a man to whom they are not married; there is no parallel term for men. Avoid.

Congressman OPTIONS: member of Congress, representative, Congressman/Congresswoman.

conman OPTIONS: con artist, rip-off artist, confidence trickster, con.

consort Use for male or female.

Cornishman This usage demonstrates that compounds with ' –man' are not gender-neutral – consider the absurd sound of 'She's a Cornishman'. Replacing such terms can require reconstructing the sentence – such as by changing 'She's/He's a Cornishman' to 'She's/He's Cornish'; or 'She's/He's from Cornwall'. For plural usage, 'the Cornish' is better than 'Cornishmen'. See topic note on page 63.
OPTIONS: Cornish, from Cornwall.

councilman OPTIONS: councillor, council member.

country squire See SQUIRE.

countrymen Keep the term in quoted historical material – eg 'friends' Romans, countrymen. . .' (but see topic note on page 84). Otherwise, balance with 'and countrywomen', usually an awkward solution, or replace.
OPTIONS: compatriots, fellow citizens; or give specific nationality – eg fellow Bulgarians. See also COMPATRIOT, FELLOW.

cow As an insult, *cow* has no parallel term applicable to men. Unlike BITCH, also one of the zooful of offensive terms likening women to animals, it is not beginning to be used for both genders. Avoid.

cowboy 1. Sometimes used gender neutrally when applied consistently to both men and women as an adjective denigrating the work of certain labourers, as in 'cowboy builders' (although, of course, this will be more often applied to men, given the composition of the building trade).
OPTIONS: second-rate, illegal, amateur, crooked, unscrupulous.
2. As for the Wild West context, use only when applying to specifically male persons; for mixed-gender groups or if the gender of the individual or group is unknown, replace.
OPTIONS: cow hand, cowherd, cow poke, cattle driver, cattle rancher, rancher, rider, range rider.

cowgirl Retain for parallel usage with COWBOY in some contexts (eg 'young cowherd' or 'young rodeo participant'). For other contexts, *cowgirl* has a patronising tone that *cowboy* lacks; in such cases, and for mixed-gender groups or if the gender of the individual or group is not known, replace. See also COWBOY. (Use OPTIONS as in COWBOY.)

craftsman OPTIONS: artisan, craft worker, artist, craftsperson, handicraft worker. Or be specific with, eg woodworker, basket weaver, potter.

craftsmanship OPTIONS: artisanry, skill, expertise, technique, work. Or be specific with, eg silverwork, stonework, carving, carpentry.

crew man OPTIONS: crew member, team member.

crumpet Has been used playfully to refer to men (as in 'Jeremy Paxman is the thinking woman's crumpet'), but is most often applied to women. One of the many descriptions included in Jane Mills' (1989) 'woman as food' list (including *tart* and *cheesecake*); see **topic note** on page 94.

cunt May be enjoying a new lease of life when used by women to refer to their genitals. Nevertheless, still widely used as a highly offensive insult toward women. See **topic note** on page 94.

currency man OPTIONS: currency dealer, foreign exchange dealer, forex dealer, currency broker.

customs man OPTIONS: customs officer/inspector/official/agent.

* * * * * * * * * * * * TOPIC NOTE * * * * * * * * * * * *

Chairman

Chairman has proved to be a stubborn term. Although it sounds masculine to most ears, it is one of the –man compounds most commonly used as a 'generic', gender-neutral term for women and men. *Chairwoman* is nearly as old as *chairman* and is often used when the subject is known to be female. When the sex of the subject is not known or specified, however, a gender-neutral term is needed.

Most gender-neutral alternatives for *chairman* have met with a great deal of opposition over the years. *Chair* is often ridiculed, though its use in this context dates back to the seventeenth century (Miller and Swift, 1989: 34). *Chairperson*, a more recent development, is another acceptable gender-neutral alternative. In practice, however, it tends to be used only for women (with *chairman* as its parallel) – especially for women who are feminists (Kramarae and Treichler, 1992: 249) – and so is not used as a true generic. It is also widely misunderstood. The assistant director general of Radio Telefís Éireann (RTE), in describing his organisation's approach to non-sexist language, claimed that 'the majority of women chairing organisations in Dublin prefer to retain the title of Chairman rather than "chairperson" on the basis that they have assumed the role as it was and not *some lower grade version of the post*' (letter to author, 1 December 1993; emphasis added). This interpretation of *chairperson* may result from the use of –person compounds as the mainstay of jokes about political correctness (*personhole, personhood*). Used carefully, however, ' –person' can be the most useful and most clearly understood alternative to ' –man' when a gender-neutral compound is needed.

If you are unhappy with any of these alternatives, there are many others from which to choose when replacing chairman – *convenor* and *moderator* are just a few. (See CHAIRMAN; topic note on page 63.)

* * * * * * * * * * * TOPIC NOTE * * * * * * * * * * * *

Church Language

In June 1992 the Methodists, Britain's largest nonconformist church, adopted proposals to eradicate the image of God as 'almost stridently male', encouraging feminine imagery such as Isaiah's comparison of God's struggles creating humankind with labour pains. Amid resistance by many members raising the spectre of thought police, the Methodists overwhelmingly supported the changes, which will result in the inclusion of alternatives to *men* and *he* in prayers and sermons and the use of *humankind* – a term, the church has noted, used more than 200 years ago in hymn translations.

In 1988, the Liturgical Commission of the General Synod of the Church of England issued a report on inclusive language in the Alternative Service Book (ASB) (*Making Women Visible*, 1988). The report offers suggestions for replacing specific non-inclusive terms and phrases within the ASB, addressing each on an individual basis so as to provide alternatives that are sensitive to context. Although the report recommends continuing with 'scriptural and traditional usage' for pronouns and adjectives referring to God (in other words, maintaining 'He', 'His', etc.), it raises a number of other issues relating to widespread exclusion of women and femaleness in church texts. Noting that many aspects of the ongoing debate on inclusive language are controversial, the Commission's report also includes current criticisms of language reform within the church (both Church of England and others). None of the suggested changes is compulsory: it is left up to individual ministers and congregations whether to implement any or all. Nevertheless, the report takes a firm stand in favour of adapting the ASB, where appropriate, in an effort 'to counterbalance the "maleness" of our existing liturgy'.

The Liturgical Commission appeared to temper its stance on inclusive language in July 1994, when the Church of England General Synod decided against replacing non-sexist terms in existing church texts. Although new texts will be written using inclusive language as much as possible, the decision falls short of embracing or encouraging such changes. The biggest fear seems to be the loss of God's masculinity; 'where possible', attempts will be made to avoid using 'he/him/his' as generic pronouns (by, for example, repeating the word 'God'), but the Liturgical Commission emphasised that it would not go so far as to refer to God as female. This step backwards reflects what some church leaders claim is a return to traditional values as reflected in traditional texts. It is no doubt part of a backlash arising in response to the church's decision to ordain women priests, which is blamed for divisions within the church and departures among members.

* *

D

daddy-longlegs OPTION: crane fly.

Dad's Army OPTION: Home Guard (unless referring to the television show by name).

dairymaid/dairyman This pair of terms is typical of the lack of parallel treatment in (roughly equivalent) job titles for men and women.
OPTIONS: dairy worker, cow milker/tender, dairy seller.

dalesman OPTIONS: dales dweller, dales inhabitant.

Dame Use only (capitalised) for the official title of a woman who has been awarded the appropriate honour or (lower case) for pantomime character. See also LADY.

daughter cell Has a specific scientific meaning (relating to cell reproduction) that should be retained.

deaconess Use *deacon* for male and female. Women have been allowed to be deacons in the Church of England since 1986 (previously, as lay members they had similar roles but were called *deaconesses*).

Dear John letter OPTIONS: break-off letter, Dear John/Jane letter.

deliveryman OPTIONS: delivery person, deliverer, courier, messenger.

de-man OPTIONS: contract, lay off/reduce the workforce, downsize.

demolition man OPTIONS: demolitionist, demolitions expert, destroyer.

dinner lady OPTIONS: cafeteria worker, canteen worker, cook, food server, kitchen assistant, school dinner preparer/server.

distaff Originally meaning 'a rod for holding flax', its association with women is rooted in the perception of spinning as women's work – not necessarily a bad thing, but it can be considered sexist (see SPINSTER). *Distaff side* (the female branch of a family) has an illuminating parallel in *spear side* (the male branch of a family). Use the term carefully.

divorcée/divorcé Avoid. If marital status is significant, use the adjectival *divorced*.

dominate Rooted in the Latin *dominus*, meaning 'master' or 'lord', so could be considered sexist. It has moved into general, gender-neutral usage, however.

don Use for male or female. From *dominus*, Latin for 'lord', so it is sometimes objected to as sexist.
OPTIONS: academic, academician, professor, head, fellow, university lecturer/teacher.

doorman OPTIONS: door attendant, porter, doorkeeper, bouncer (as in a nightclub – although some in the profession object to the 'heavy' connotations of this term), security guard.

Doris An insulting term used among police to refer to some female colleagues; abolished by Metropolitan Police in a 1992 directive on language use among its members.

doubting Thomas Named for the sceptical apostle, so its retention can be justified on the grounds of historical accuracy.
OPTIONS: doubter, sceptic.

dragoman Not a sexist term etymologically; it is rooted in the Arabic for 'interpreter'.

draughtsman As with FISHERMAN/FISHER, can easily be replaced with the root form plus ' –er' suffix, dropping the gender. One who fishes is a *fisher*; one who drafts is a *draughter* (sometimes *drafter*).
OPTIONS: draughter/drafter, draughtsperson, designer, technical artist.

draughtsmanship OPTIONS: drafting ability/skills, drawing ability.

dukedom OPTION: duchy.

dumb blonde Like BIMBO, this term has no real male parallel ('dumb blond', like 'toyboy' or 'bimboy', is sometimes used for men, but men are not labelled in this way as frequently as are women). It perpetuates a sexist stereotype and thus should be avoided.

dustman OPTIONS: refuse collector, garbage collector.

Dutchman This usage demonstrates that compounds with' –man' are not gender-neutral – consider the absurd sound of 'She's a Dutchman'. Replacing such terms can require reconstructing the sentence – such as by changing 'She's/He's a Dutchman' to 'She's/He's Dutch', etc. For plural usage, 'the Dutch' is better than 'Dutchmen'. See **topic note** on page 63.

OPTIONS: Dutch person, Dutch, Netherlander; if appropriate, be more specific, eg Hollander.

dyke Like BITCH, this term is being reclaimed by some lesbians as a positive label, though it is still used as an insult to refer to 'unfeminine' lesbians by others. Use carefully.

E

earth mother No parallel term for men exists, which is probably one reason it has taken on sometimes derogatory connotations. Use only in a gender-specific sense, or replace with a gender-neutral term usable for men or women and sensitive to context.
OPTIONS: earth mother/earth father, down-to-earth type, unpretentious type, fertile parent/woman/man, nature lover.

educatress See topic note on page 26.
OPTIONS: educator, teacher.

effeminate A sexist term that associates femininity with weakness and passivity. If that is what is meant, replace with an alternative that is gender-neutral.
OPTIONS: weak, passive, soft, delicate, timid, flowery, chintzy.

emancipate Not a sexist term; it derives from the Latin *emancipare*, meaning 'free of parental control'.

emasculate There is no female equivalent – compare EFFEMINATE (an adjective as opposed to a verb), which has a quite different meaning. See also UNMAN.
1. OPTIONS: disarm, disempower, incapacitate, muzzle, paralyse, handcuff, weaken.
2. OPTION: castrate (but use only in its literal sense).

empress *Emperor* can be used for a male or female empire-ruler. Use *empress* for the wife of an emperor when she does not share power equally.

Englishman This usage demonstrates that compounds with ' –man' are not gender-neutral – consider the absurd sound of 'She's an Englishman'. Replacing such terms can require reconstructing the sentence – such as by changing 'She's/He's an Englishman' to 'She's/ He's English'. For plural usage, 'the English' is better than 'Englishmen'. See topic note on page 63.
OPTIONS: an English person, English, the English; depending on context, British or Briton might be appropriate.

'An Englishman's home is his castle' This phrase is not easy to rectify without, some would say, spoiling the flavour, but behind the quaintness of the saying is a dangerously reactionary belief that has been used countless times to justify, among other things, domestic violence. Replace, unless using to emphasise the point that an Englishman's home is considered to be sacrosant.

OPTIONS: one's home is one's castle, an English person's home is a castle, the sanctity of the home.

esquire (Esq) A 'respectful' title used only for men. It no longer relates to a specific honour, degree or profession (although in the US it is used for lawyers of either sex). Avoid.

Essex girl/Essex man An example of unparallel treatment ('girl' versus 'man') in supposedly parallel terms for men and women. Promotes a stereotype that is offensive to many people from or who live in Essex, so best avoided. If retaining, use *Essex woman* and *Essex man*.

every man for himself OPTIONS: everyone for themselves, everyone for him- and herself.

Everyman OPTIONS: ordinary person, average person, citizen. See also JOE PUBLIC, JOE BLOGGS.

exciseman OPTIONS: excise officer/inspector/official/agent/collector.

executrix OPTIONS: executor, administrator.

expatriate Often shortened to *ex-pat*, this term has its root in the Latin for 'native land', which is related to that for 'father', but it has for the most part lost its gender-specific meaning.

OPTIONS: exile, émigré, resident in a foreign country.

* * * * * * * * * * * * TOPIC NOTE * * * * * * * * * * * *

' –ess' and ' –ette' Words

When added to perfectly acceptable, gender-neutral words like *author*, *poet* and *manager*, these feminising suffixes (along with ' –trix', ' –ine' and ' –enne') contribute to a perception that the male is the standard form and the female is the subset. The use of –ess and –ette suffixes, in particular, suggests that the female is somehow less important than the male. (In fact, the first definition given for –ette in *Collins' English Dictionary* is 'small: *cigarette*; *kitchenette*'.) Not only are they disparaging and often facetious, but they are unnecessary. In most cases in which –ess and –ette endings are used, the gender of the person referred to is not important. If it is, it can be specified with a straightforward modifier: male author, female poet. (Be careful, however, that these are used in a balanced way – avoid saying, for instance, 'one poet and one female poet'.)

Many people consider some of these forms more objectionable than others. On the 'reasonable' end of the scale, for example, may be found *actress*; at the opposite extreme may be terms that are both sexist and racist such as *Jewess* and *Negress*. Nevertheless, all are formed in the same way and indicate subsets, or less important groups, of a larger group that is considered the standard. The term *actor*, for example, is to be found in the name of the profession's trade organisation (British Actors' Equity Association, so-called since its founding and intended to represent both male and female actors); as well as in the names of smaller groups and venues such as Actors' Playhouse. *Actress* is never used in this way.

Generally, use the root form (*author*, *poet*, *heir*) of all these terms for both male and female; avoid the suffixes. For many of these terms, the male and female versions have quite different meanings: *heir/heiress*, *governor/governess*, *steward/stewardess*, *priest/priestess*. In these pairs, the feminine version will often need to be replaced by an entirely different term – for example, *tutor* or *private instructor* for *governess*. The terms *prince* and *princess* should be retained only when referring to royal personages. In other contexts ('fit for a prince', a 'princess telephone'), they have quite different meanings and can usually be replaced with gender-neutral terms (see PRINCE; PRINCESS). Other examples of unparallel use are *god* and *goddess*. These should be used in a fair and balanced way in sex-specific contexts (such as Greek mythology or in reference to goddess-based religions) (see GOD/GODDESS).

The –ess suffix used for the feminine of some animal names (such as *lioness* and *tigress*) is no less sexist; it serves to make the female of the species the odd one out. Consider the many ways these animal names are used in everyday sayings ('the lion's share', 'to have a tiger by the tail') and in common terms (tiger lily, tiger's eye); then compare *tigress*'s second meaning – that of a wild, fierce, or sexually aggressive woman. As with job descriptions for humans, the suffix used in animal names is unnecessary (*Collins' English Dictionary*, for example, does not define *lion* or *tiger* as specifically male). Use the same form for male or female; if distinguishing the gender is important, use *male lion* or *female tiger*.

In the debate about ordaining women in the Church of England, it is interesting to note that those in favour refer to women as *priests*; many of those opposed, however, use *priestesses*, with the intention of diminishing the role and highlighting what they perceive as the absurdity of the notion. One opponent, for example, clarified this distinction when she expressed her pleasure in the patriarchal nature of Christianity: 'The Jewish and Christian message was to raise humanity above the naturalistic cults of fertility, with their pantheism and often murky and secretive ceremonial practices, in which priestesses played such a major part' (*Guardian*, 7 November 1992) (see PRIEST; PRIESTESS).

* *

F

fair/fairer sex OPTION: women.

fairy Not necessarily a sexist term, as it can be used for male or female supernatural beings. Many familiar fairies, however, are female (*fairy godmother*, *fairy princess*); when either sex is intended, replace with a gender-neutral term. Otherwise, use for male or female (but not for gay men).

fairy godmother OPTIONS: fairy godparent, benefactor, guardian angel, fairy godmother/fairy godfather.

fallen woman An outdated concept as well as term. Avoid. See also PROSTITUTE.

fall guy See GUY.
OPTIONS: scapegoat, dupe, mug, sucker, easy mark, con victim.

family man Used to describe a certain type of man who is concerned with family and home, as opposed to a man concerned more with work or 'outside' interests. It has no parallel for women, as the assumption is that all women are 'family women'. Sexist and clichéd.

fanny A commonly used but, for many women, unsatisfactory term for *vagina* or women's genitalia. (In the US it refers to the bottom or backside and is used for both sexes.) Many women object because it is too cute and mild. Other terms are used often as insults (eg *cunt*) or seem too clinical (eg *vagina*). See topic note on page 94.

farmer's wife A woman married to a farmer is in most cases a *farmer* herself, unless she has another occupation by which she wants to be known. This construction, used in many other contexts as well ('the neighbour and his wife', 'the world and his wife'), serves to denigrate women to the position of household pet or appliance. Avoid.

father (noun) 1. Use strictly in the sense of 'male parent' or for a member of the clergy.
2. When referring to God, a number of gender-neutral alternatives could be used. Usually this is a very personal choice.
OPTIONS: Creator, Almighty, God, Holy One.
3. Replace when used in the sense of 'founder', even if the subject is male. The terms *father* and *mother* have very different connotations and so are not used in a balanced way for this meaning. Note the

absurd sound of, for example, 'Curie is the mother of radioactivity' as opposed to 'Faraday is the father of electricity'.
OPTIONS: founder, inventor, originator, source.

father (verb) 'To father' has a very different meaning from 'to mother'; according to Collins' English Dictionary, it means 'to beget; to create, found, originate, etc.' as opposed to 'to give birth to or produce; to nurture, protect, etc.' Be careful not to use the term in a way that perpetuates sexist and outdated stereotypes of parenting roles. See also MOTHER (verb).
OPTIONS: parent, nurture, create, procreate, reproduce, found, invent, originate.

father of the chapel OPTIONS: shop steward, union leader, representative, union supervisor, mother of the chapel/father of the chapel.

fatherland Unless using in its historical sense (especially of Germany as the 'Fatherland'), replace. See also MOTHERLAND.
OPTIONS: home country, native land, homeland, homeground, the old country, birthplace.

Father Time OPTION: time.

fellow/fellowship Etymologically not a sexist term. It derives from the Old Norse for 'one who lays down money' and was used historically in relation to joint ventures and financial associations. It is nevertheless sometimes objected to as a masculine term which brings to mind male images ('The fellow stood waving a hat', for example, clearly refers to a man) and which promotes an 'old boy network' from which women are excluded ('I had a drink with the fellas'). Be careful, then, in how you use it.
1. When used in an inclusive, gender-neutral way, or for both sexes, retain – for example, in 'Well, she's a jolly good fellow'.
2. In the sense of 'friend' or 'chap', it can be replaced with a less masculine-sounding term. See also GUY.
OPTIONS: companion, partner, associate, friend; companionship, friendship, camaraderie, association, harmony, communion.
3. In the academic sense, 'fellow' and 'fellowship' must usually be retained in their specific senses and are used gender-neutrally ('She was made a Fellow of the Royal Society').
OPTIONS: scholar, student, associate, special member, award recipient; scholarship, award, honorarium, merit grant.

fellow traveller OPTIONS: travelling companion, sympathiser.

female Not a sexist term. It derives from *femella*, Latin for 'little woman', and until the seventeenth century was spelled *femal* or *femall*. Its spelling was changed as it became associated with *male*.

For many centuries the word had negative connotations, suggesting inferiority and even non-humanness, and although today it is sometimes considered derogatory and passed over for 'woman' as a modifier, it is generally not considered offensive. As a noun, though, in most contexts it retains its sense of non-humanness and is used mostly in relation to animals or statistics.

feminine/femininity Like *female*, this derives from the Latin for 'woman'. It has been subjected to sexist use, however, by being associated with weakness or inferiority; in music and linguistics, for instance, it is used to describe weak or unstressed beats, syllables, or rhymes. See WOMANISH.

feminist Often used in a derogatory sense, as in 'I'm not a rabid feminist', or as an insult to describe a strong, assertive woman, sometimes called a 'man-hater'. Its use as a disparaging term may explain why many women are reluctant to identify themselves as feminists. Use strictly for someone who advocates women's rights. Keep in mind, however, that many women argue that men cannot be feminists.

femme fatale Has no parallel for men, and is further sexist in that it is based on the stereotype of women as temptresses. Replace with a specific term describing the behaviour.
OPTIONS: heartbreaker, seducer, dangerous woman.

fiancé/fiancée Use *fiancé* for male or female, or replace.
OPTIONS: girlfriend/boyfriend, betrothed, partner, lover, future husband/future wife.

fireman OPTIONS: firefighter, fire crew member.

First Lady Use the person's name when referring to the spouse (so far, all have been wives) of the US president. Hillary Rodham Clinton opted to be referred to as 'the Presidential Partner'.

fisherman *Fisher* has quite a long and respected history.
OPTIONS: fisher, angler; in adjectival use, *fishing* is often adequate ('a row of fishing cottages').

fishwife Do not use to describe a woman who swears; it is sexist to consider such behaviour 'unladylike' for women but acceptable for men.
OPTIONS: fishmonger, fish seller.

flagman OPTIONS: flag waver, flagger, signaller.

flash boy/flash Harry OPTIONS: show-off, exhibitionist, hotshot.

flower girl In the sense of a member of a wedding party, this usage is not sexist as it refers to a young person who in other contexts would also be considered a 'girl'. In other senses of the word, replace.
OPTIONS: flower seller, flower vendor, florist, flower stall owner.

forefather OPTIONS: forebear, ancestor, precursor, forerunner.

foreman OPTIONS: supervisor, team leader, work leader.

foreplay Be careful how this is used. Women and men experience the 'phases' of sexual intercourse very differently. Although most people know what is meant by the word, the use of *foreplay* to describe the activity before penetration assumes that penetration is the be-all and end-all of heterosexual intercourse. Better to use specific terms and to avoid entirely the emphasis on pre- or post-penetration. See also topic note on page 94.
OPTIONS: kissing, petting, caressing, fondling, oral sex, cunnilingus, fellatio.

founding fathers OPTIONS: founders (sometimes capitalised), colonists, first settlers, pioneers.

fraternal twins OPTION: non-identical twins.

fraternity Use only for specifically male-only groups, such as 'Greek' societies on university campuses in the US (with *sorority* as the counterpart for women). When used in the context of male/female grouping or gender neutrally, replace. See also BROTHERHOOD.
OPTIONS: community, family, friendship, humanity, sibship, alliance, federation, grouping, league.

fratricide Unless using in its specific, literal sense – that of 'brother killing' – or its specific military sense – that of 'nuclear missile destruction' – replace with a gender-neutral term.
OPTIONS: internal struggle, internecine warfare.

freedman OPTIONS: freed slave, former slave.

freeman OPTIONS: citizen, free citizen. 'Freewoman' was used in the feminist movement and was the title of a British weekly feminist review published in 1911–12 (Maggio, 1988: 49).

Frenchman This usage demonstrates that compounds with ' –man' are not gender-neutral – consider the absurd sound of 'She's a Frenchman'. Replacing such terms can require reconstructing the sentence – such as by changing 'She's/He's a Frenchman' to 'She's/He's French', etc. For plural usage, 'the French' is better then 'Frenchmen'. See topic note on page 63.

OPTIONS: a French person, French.

freshman OPTIONS: fresher, first-year student.

frigid A sexist and insulting label used for women who cannot achieve orgasm, but most often used to describe any woman considered sexually unresponsive or unavailable (to men for penetrative sex). Ironically, it originally was applied to both men and women. Now, its male 'equivalent', *impotent*, does not carry any connotations of neurosis, is not applied to a man who has chosen not to have penetrative sex, and is often (although not always) treated by doctors as a purely physiological problem. Avoid *frigid*.

frogman OPTIONS: frog diver, diver, police diver, scuba diver, underwater explorer.

frontiersman OPTIONS: pioneer, frontiersperson, frontier dweller.

front man OPTIONS: figurehead, front, nominal head, deputy, spokesperson, puppet.

G

gamesman OPTIONS: gamester, gambler, player.

gamesmanship OPTIONS: competition, rivalry, fair play, expertise, cunning, artifice, guile.

gasman OPTIONS: gas board worker, meter reader, gas line installer.

gentleman Use only in formal addresses ('Ladies and Gentleman') where a more appropriate term ('Friends', 'My Fellow Editors') cannot be found (but see also FELLOW).
1. In the sense of a person with manners ('He's a perfect gentleman'), rearrange the sentence if necessary to say what you mean.
OPTIONS: he has perfect manners/is extremely polite/is gentle/is courteous.

gentleman's agreement OPTIONS: informal agreement, honourable agreement, handshake agreement, verbal agreement, unwritten agreement.

gentleman-farmer If necessary to use for historical accuracy, put *gentleman* in quotation marks to signal that the term as used might be offensive not only to women but to those farmers who by exclusion are considered 'ungentlemanly'.
OPTIONS: 'gentleman'-farmer, farm owner, casual farmer, weekend farmer.

gigolo OPTIONS: prostitute, kept man.

gingerbread man Supermarket workers have relabelled packages as 'gingerbread persons', causing outrage among traditionalists and the National Association of Master Bakers (*Guardian*, 22 January 1994).
OPTIONS: gingerbread person/figure, gingerbread woman/gingerbread man; (plural): gingerbread folk/people/figures, gingerbread women and gingerbread men.

girl Be careful of the context in which you use this term. Use it, for example, where you would use *boy* for the male counterpart, unless that too is derogatory, as in *best boy*, a (usually adult) member of a film crew. Generally, girls are *girls* up to 13–16 years old; after that they are (*young*) *women*.

girl Friday/Man Friday An example of unparallel treatment ('girl' versus 'man') in supposedly parallel terms for women and men (*Man Friday* comes from Daniel Defoe's *Robinson Crusoe*). The archetypal *girl Friday*, the character Lois Lane (from *Superman*), is a grown woman. Replace with a gender-neutral term.

OPTIONS: assistant, right hand, aide, manager, office junior, secretary, helper.

God/god The term can be used for female or male figures in monotheistic religions. See also FATHER. In other contexts, use only in a sex-specific sense where you would use *goddess* as the female equivalent. See GODDESS; topic note on page 26.

goddess 1. Use when referring to goddess-oriented religions or mythologies, or where *goddess* carries equal weight with *god* in multiple-deity religions. See GOD; topic note on page 26.
2. If using to refer to a woman considered sexually attractive, use only where you would also use *god* for the male equivalent – eg 'a screen goddess'.

golden girl OPTIONS: rising star, bright star.

governess Retain for its specific meaning in historical contexts. See topic note on page 26.
OPTIONS: live-in child carer, live-in teacher, live-in instructor, nanny.

governor Use for male or female head of a school, state or organisation. Not parallel with GOVERNESS. See topic note on page 26.

granddad/granddaddy For the sense of the greatest or oldest – as in 'London Underground is the granddad of urban transport systems', replace.
OPTIONS: pioneer, first, greatest, largest, oldest, ideal, height, pinnacle.

grandfather clause OPTION: grandparent clause.

grandfather clock OPTIONS: longcase clock, standing clock.

grandfatherly/grandmotherly Watch how these are used; they often carry unparallel and stereotypical connotations. *Collins' English Dictionary*, for example, elaborates on its definition of *grandfatherly* with '. . . esp. in being kindly'. Under *grandmotherly*, it has '. . . esp. in being protective, indulgent or solicitous'.

granny bond OPTION: retirement issue certificate.

granny dress OPTIONS: Victorian-style dress, old-fashioned dress.

granny flat OPTIONS: grannex (from 'granny annexe'), self-contained flat, caretaker's flat, rental flat.

granny knot OPTION: unstable reef knot.

Granny Smith Not a sexist term. The apple is named after its first producer, Maria Ann Smith, a nineteenth-century Australian.

groomsman OPTION: groom's attendant.

groundsman OPTIONS: gardener, caretaker, maintenance worker, parks worker, grounds keeper.

groupie Usually applied, in a derogatory sense, to female fans, though it is not gender specific and can be applied to women and men both.

guildsman OPTIONS: artisan, guildsperson, guild member.

gunman 1. OPTIONS: shooter, terrorist, sharpshooter, hired killer, assassin.
2. (Wild West context) OPTIONS: gunfigher, gunslinger.

guy In the US *guy* is often applied equally to women and men; it probably derives from American use of *guy* from Guy Fawkes and may have first been used in the early 1800s. Here it is generally used only for men, a synonym for *chap* or, sometimes, FELLOW.

H

handmaiden 1. (human) OPTIONS: servant, attendant.
2. (non-human) OPTIONS: instrument, agent, vehicle, lesser partner.

handyman OPTIONS: repair person, caretaker, odd-jobber, general worker, grounds keeper.

hangman OPTION: executioner.

harlot OPTION: prostitute.

harvestman OPTION: harvester.

he Often used as a false generic: *he* does not stand for *he/she*, any more than *she* does. See **topic note** on page 79.

headmaster/headmistress An old-fashioned sounding usage that seems to be gradually slipping out of use. Although *headmaster* is one of the few –master compound words used gender specifically, its 'counterpart', *headmistress*, suffers from the illicit and sexual connotations of MISTRESS as used today. Replace with less imbalanced, gender-neutral terms, as is increasingly being done in the educational community. See also MASTER.
OPTIONS: head teacher, head, principal, rector.

heiress Has a meaning distinct from 'female heir', with connotations of glamour and pampered lifestyle. Use *heir* for male or female inheritor. See also **topic note** on page 26. OPTIONS: heir, inheritor, successor.

hell hath no fury like a woman scorned A sexist saying of dubious accuracy, suggesting that women have a unique response to being rejected. Avoid.

helmsman OPTIONS: pilot, navigator, steerer, guide, guider, cox.

henchman OPTIONS: faithful attendant, assistant, right-hand assistant, sidekick, associate, accomplice, hanger-on, lackey, minion.

hen party This, and its counterpart STAG PARTY, are both sexist in the associations made by their animal imagery. Many terms associate women with hens and with what are considered hen-like qualities; fussy, obedient, silly, timid, bossy. Replace.
OPTIONS: bride's party, pre-wedding party, last-chance party.

37

henpecked Replace, and use alternatives only when appropriate for a man in the same way as for a woman.
OPTIONS: nagged (but see NAG), browbeaten, downtrodden, dominated (but see DOMINATE), bullied, scolded.

hersdman OPTIONS: herder, cattle breeder.

heroine OPTIONS: hero, protagonist, central character, lead, principle, brave person. The American writer Maya Angelou has offered *sheroe*.

herstory A word play on HISTORY (not itself a sexist term) used to describe the past as seen through women's eyes and to highlight women's achievements as opposed to male-dominated history as traditionally taught. Not in common use in mainstream publications, but frequently used in feminist publications. Not intended to be a synonym for HISTORY. See also **topic note** on page 41.

history Not a sexist term (from the Greek word *historia*). See also HERSTORY.

hit man OPTIONS: contract killer, hired assassin, hired gun, assassin, murderer.

homo- This prefix is not sexist; it derives from the Greek for 'equal'.

homosexuals Watch how the term is used; it often has a male-only connotation.
OPTIONS: lesbians and gay men, gays.

horseman OPTIONS: horse rider, equestrian, horseback rider, horseman/horsewoman.

horsemanship OPTIONS: horse-riding skill/ability, horse-handling skill/ability/technique, equestrianism, equitation.

host/hostess Use *host*, whether male or female. See **topic note** on page 26.

househusband Objected to for the same reasons as HOUSEWIFE, though it has a very different sense and is used generally tongue in cheek. Replace.
OPTIONS: homemaker, home worker, consumer, house holder; some market researchers have begun to use *main shopper*.

houseman OPTIONS: house officer (official position); in a more generic sense, use intern or resident.

housewife Inaccurate (many are in fact men) and offensive ('married to a house?'), although it may be being reclaimed by women as a positive label.
OPTIONS: homemaker, home worker, consumer, house holder; some market researchers have begun to use *main shopper*.

human Not a sexist term. Related to the Latin *humus*, meaning 'earth', and probably meant 'earthly beings'.

huntsman OPTIONS: hunter, hunt leader.

husbandry OPTIONS: farming, agriculture, tillage, animal breeding, cultivation.

* * * * * * * * * * * * TOPIC NOTE * * * * * * * * * * * *

Honorifics: Miss, Mrs and Ms

Originally, the honorifics (also called courtesy titles) Miss and Mrs distinguished between young women (and girls) and mature women, without reference to marital status. In the past hundred years the titles have come to refer to marital status: the use of Miss and Mrs has allowed writers and speakers to distinguish between unmarried and married women, something that has not been considered necessary regarding men. (*Master* may be considered a *Miss* form for men, but it is rarely used today; when it is, it more likely refers to young boys, not to all unmarried men.) Efforts to do away with this distinction have a long history and include using no titles at all and inventing new forms of address. The enduring invention, however, is *Ms*.

Although it is not known when *Ms* was devised, it seems to have first come into widespread use in 1950s' America in business correspondence, where its use was advised by secretarial manuals. *Ms* was particularly useful in business because it allowed letter writers to address their correspondence personally even when the addressee's marital status was not known.

Complaints about *Ms* as a term – and reluctance to adopt

it as stylistic practice – generally focus on the sound of the word, which some find objectionable (*mizz*, sounding to some like a lazy pronunciation of *miss*) and on the fact that it appears as an abbreviation but has no unabbreviated form. Such objections, however, are overruled by the practicality of the term, even for those who have no personal objection to the *Miss/Mrs* distinction. The term is now fairly widely used in the business community and in mainstream, as well as feminist, periodicals.

Ms should be used as the parallel of *Mr*. Where no titles are used, such as when referring by last name only (as often on sports pages, do not use them for women or men. When using professional titles, such as *Dr*, do not use courtesy titles. When using courtesy titles, use *Ms* as you would *Mr*. Some women prefer using *Miss* or *Mrs*, and if such a preference is expressed, it should be followed.

* *

ice cream man OPTIONS: ice cream vendor/seller.

illegitimate Do not use to refer to a child whose father is not known or not married to its mother; it is outdated to refer to children of unmarried parents as 'not legitimate'. Furthermore, it is sexist to suggest that 'legitimacy' requires a married mother and father; many women choose to have children on their own or with a partner who is not the child's father. If parenthood details are necessary, use 'child of unmarried parents'. See also SINGLE MOTHER.
OPTIONS: child of unmarried parents, child of lone parent.

infantryman OPTIONS: foot soldier, enlisted soldier.

instructress OPTION: instructor. See **topic note** on page 26.

insurance man OPTIONS: insurance agent, insurance seller/vendor/rep.

intuition See WOMEN'S INTUITION.

Irishman This usage demonstrates that compounds with ' –man' are not gender-neutral – consider the absurd sound of 'She's an Irishman'. Replacing such terms can require reconstructing the sentence – such as by changing 'She's/He's an Irishman' to 'She's/He's Irish'. For plural usage, 'the Irish' is better than 'Irishmen'. See **topic note** on page 63.
OPTIONS: an Irish person, Irish, person from Ireland. If appropriate, be more specific – eg Dubliner.

Isle of Man Do not change. See also MANXMAN.

* * * * * * * * * * * * TOPIC NOTE * * * * * * * * * * * *

Innovations: New Words

Some words are objected to for their sexist sound or appearance, even if this contrasts with the known etymology of the word – its roots or origin – which may have nothing to do with masculinity or sexism. Often the sound of the word – or perhaps its meaning or the way it is used – is seen to contribute to sexist perceptions.

To combat this, many feminist writers have coined woman-based terms as alternatives or to supplement male-based language. Such coinages include *herstory, ovular* (contrasted with *seminal,* related to 'semen/seed'), *himmicane* (as opposed to *hurricane*), *hersterectomy, womage* (as opposed to *manage*), *efemcipated, ovarimony* (as opposed to *testimony*), *testaria* (based on *hysteria* and used for 'the state of being unemotional'), and *wimmin/womyn.* Many of these are playful; all are meant to alert readers to the sexism inherent in the English language. Coining women-based terms is not trading one form of sexism for another; many of these terms are not actually synonyms that are intended to replace the male-based term, but are new words with their own, new meaning. *Herstory,* for example, is not another word for *history*; it refers to the often untold story of women's achievements and contributions.

Writers can use this new vocabulary as a resource. In some cases, these terms can be used to highlight a sexist practice (the use of *himmicane* drew attention to the fact that hurricanes were always named after women, and may have helped bring about the change to alternating male and female names for hurricanes) or to convey a new meaning (as in *herstory*). When using such terms, be sensitive to the audience by explaining a new term where readers are likely to be unfamiliar with it.

* *

J

jack– Words and phrases beginning or ending in –jack are not usually sexist. Although most derive from the man's name John, these terms have generally come to be used in a gender-neutral sense: bootjack, jack-in-the-box, Union Jack. Be sensitive to context.

I'm all right, Jack Usually applies to women and men (an 'I'm all right Jack' attitude) and so can be considered non-sexist.
OPTIONS: complacency, smugness.

Jewess Use Jew (but only if religion is relevant). See topic note on page 26.

Joe Bloggs OPTIONS: average person, Jane Bloggs or Joe Bloggs, punter, typical consumer/reader/viewer, average citizen.

Joe Public OPTIONS: average person, Jane Public or Joe Public, punter, typical consumer/reader/viewer, average citizen.

Johnny come lately OPTIONS: newcomer, upstart, new arrival, rookie.

journeyman OPTIONS: certified craftworker, skilled worker, trainee, apprentice.

jury foreman OPTIONS: jury representative, jury spokesperson.

* * * * * * * * * * * * **TOPIC NOTE** * * * * * * * * * * * *

Journalism

Moves toward non-sexist language use in newspapers are a visible indication of the changes being made today. People are greatly influenced by what they see daily in print. But language reform in journalism is actually slower than in other sectors of society. Newspapers tend to be wave-riders rather than trend-setters, safely using only terms that have found their way into current use.

Style guides of individual newspapers give clues about those papers' policies (or lack of them) on sexist language. The

Guardian has no specific guidelines governing sexist language; yet it purports to have an established understanding among reporters and sub-editors that sexist language is not acceptable. The assumption that everyone hired by the paper will interpret 'sexist' in the same way means that whatever informal policy exists is not consistently implemented; *poetess, firemen, servicemen and their wives* are among the terms that have recently slipped by into print. The Times' style guide (*The Times*, 1992) states that its aim in addressing sexist language is to avoid giving offence to women while also avoiding the destruction of idiom. In particular, the guide specifies that courtesy titles should be used, but that *Ms* should be used only when requested, not as a matter of course. The *Independent*'s style guide (*Independent*, 1992) advises the opposite: to use *Ms* unless otherwise specified. Both these guides also prohibit the use of what *The Times* calls 'bisexual' pronouns (using *he* for he/she), and feminine endings on such words as *authoress* and *poetess*, which *The Times* points out 'should be avoided as unnecessary'. Both papers, however, believe *actress* is necessary to retain, as it is, according to the *Independent*, unavoidable.

The National Union of Journalists (NUJ), on the other hand, takes a more sweeping approach in its guidelines for promoting equality through journalism, produced by the NUJ's Equality Council (NUJ, 'Images of Women: Guidelines for Promoting Equality through Journalism', 1986). The object of the guidelines is 'to show how everyday words and phrases help to form and perpetuate a discriminatory, patronising attitude towards women'. The union also issues a one-page style guide offering alternatives to sexist words and phrases (NUJ, 'Equality Style Guide', n.d.). Both documents cite the code of conduct for journalists: 'A journalist shall neither originate nor process material which encourages discrimination on grounds of race, colour, creed, gender or sexual orientation.'

* *

K

key-man assurance OPTIONS: executive assurance, key executive assurance.

king (noun) Use only in its literal sense for a male monarch. See also CHESS; QUEEN.
OPTIONS: ruler, monarch, sovereign, leader, figurehead, chief.

king (adj) As a modifier or prefix (as in 'king prawn' or 'kingpin'), this term is sexist because the female 'equivalent', *queen*, is not used in the same manner. Some terms incorporating *king* are generally not considered sexist or are acceptable only because a nonsexist synonym that would be clearly understood by all is not available (such as *kingfisher*). Many others are replaceable, however, and wherever possible should be replaced.
OPTIONS: royal, ruling, regal; top, leading, chief, main; large, largest, greatest, outsize.

kingdom OPTIONS: empire, monarchy, land, realm, region, territory, fief.

kingdom come OPTIONS: the next world, the end of the world, life after death, eternal life, oblivion, eternity, paradise.

kingly The female 'equivalent', *queenly*, has a very different connotation.
OPTIONS: royal, regal, majestic, monarchical.

king of the castle OPTIONS: keeper of the castle, monarch of the mountain, ruler of the roost.

king salmon OPTION: Chinook salmon.

king-size OPTIONS: large, extra large, jumbo, outsize.

kinsman OPTIONS: kin, relation, family member, sibling, kinswoman/kinsman.

knight Although both women and men are knighted, only men are *knights*; knighted women are DAMES. See also CHESS; LADY.

knight in shining armour Although the original idea behind this term – that a damsel in distress needs a knightly saviour – is generally sexist, these days the role can be filled by someone of either sex, and the term is usually used ironically. Unless using in its most literal sense, replace with a gender-neutral term.

OPTIONS: saviour, fairy godparent, rescuer, hero.

L

ladies' fingers/lady's finger OPTIONS: okra, bhindi.

ladies' man The term and the notion behind it are both sexist. Also, the female 'equivalents' are generally negative – *man-eater, femme fatale* – or derogatory – *slut, whore, slag*. Replace with a gender-neutral term to be used fairly with men or women.
OPTIONS: philanderer, heartbreaker.

ladies' room/the ladies' OPTIONS: women's room, toilet, lavatory.

lady 1. Never use as an adjective before, for example, job titles or occupations ('lady lawyer') or positions ('Lady Chairman').
2. Use if also using parallel *gentleman* ('Ladies and gentlemen'), but not in isolation ('ladies, ladies. . .').
3. Use when referring to a female member of the House of Lords. See LORD.
4. Many terms incorporating *lady* are generally not considered sexist or are acceptable only because a nonsexist synonym that would be clearly understood by all is not available (*ladybird, ladyfinger*). Wherever possible, replace.

lady bountiful Although based on a fictional female character (in George Farquhar's *The Beaux' Strategem* of 1707), the term as used now in a gender-neutral sense could be considered sexist. It usually carries negative connotations, so the alternatives may not be appropriate for all contexts.
OPTIONS: benefactor, charitable person, generous person, donor, sponsor, bestower, patron (but see PATRON).

lady finger OPTIONS: sponge cake, finger-shaped cake.

lady-in-waiting Use only in specific sense for that member of the royal household.
OPTIONS: attendant, helper, servant.

lady-killer An offensive notion as well as term. See LADIES' MAN.

ladylike Not everyone associates the same characteristics with being a 'lady'. Better to use specific terms to mean what you say.
OPTIONS: polite, elegant, courteous, generous, soft-spoken, refined, gentle, posh, delicate, frail, sensitive.

lady luck OPTIONS: luck, good fortune.

landlord/landlady The terms *landlord* and *landlady* have very different connotations: one is common parlance for a property owner; the other conjures up images of a nosy older woman in slippers. Because the terms *lord* and *lady* are still used (and in obviously gender-based ways), it is difficult to apply *lord* to both sexes as a neutral term, as has been attempted in the US. When able to be more specific, replace with an option.
OPTIONS: owner, lessor, freeholder, land owner, landholder, proprietor, rent collector, leaseholder. The *Guardian*'s Marcel Berlins has suggested using *landor*.

landsman 1. OPTIONS: land dweller, land lover, land lubber.
2. OPTIONS: fellow citizen, fellow (insert name of place or country) (but see FELLOW), compatriot (but see COMPATRIOT), neighbour.

laundress OPTIONS: launderer, clothes washer, laundry worker.

laundryman/laundrywoman OPTIONS: laundry collector/deliverer, laundry worker.

lazy Susan OPTIONS: revolving tray, revolving relish server.

layman OPTIONS: layperson, non-expert, average reader, viewer, member of the laity.

leading lady Use *leading woman* for parallel use with *leading man*; otherwise replace.
OPTIONS: lead, star, featured performer, starring partner, actor.

lengthman OPTIONS: road repairer, road worker, railway worker, road/track maintenance worker.

leopardess See topic note on page 26.
OPTION: leopard.

leprechaun Use for male and female, although they are usually considered to be male. The word means 'little body'.

liftman OPTIONS: lift operator, lift attendant.

like a man Not everyone associates the same characteristics with 'taking it like a man'. Better to use specific terms to mean what you say. Always replace with a gender-neutral term when applying to women or a mixed-sex group.
OPTIONS: squarely, without breaking down, courageously, bravely, straight.

lioness See topic note on page 26.
OPTION: lion.

liveryman Members of the City of London's livery companies are called *liverymen* (or *freemen* in some cases), whether they are male or female. This is not likely to change; although one-quarter of the solicitors' company membership is women, for example, there has been no discussion of the use of *liverywoman* or a gender-neutral term. In some cases, it is possible to avoid the term by using 'livery company member'.

Lolita The concept behind this term (derived from a character in a Vladimir Nabokov novel, but since used as a generic term) is itself offensive. A young woman who is sexually active is simply that; a very young woman (or girl) who is considered desirable or even flirtatious should not be labelled. Instead, label the man (usually older) who harbours sexual thoughts about young girls. See NYMPHET, NYMPHOMANIA.

lollipop lady An example of unparallel usage; the male equivalent is a *lollipop man*.
OPTIONS: lollipop woman/lollipop man, school crossing patrol officer.

longshoreman OPTIONS: docker, dockworker, wharfhand, stevedore.

lord 1. Like KING, *lord* used as a generic term (as a prefix meaning 'superior', for example) is usually sexist; its female 'counterpart', LADY, is used very differently. Replace where possible. See also LANDLORD/LANDLADY.
2. Retain in official titles (Lord Chief Justice, Lord Mayor) and in honorary titles (for members of the peerage). *Lord* is often used to include women and men, especially where the original meaning included only men but women have since joined: House of Lords (and Ladies), for instance. Presumably a female head of the judiciary would also be called Lord Chancellor.
3. Replace when using to refer to God. See FATHER; GOD.
OPTIONS: Almighty, Creator, Holy One, God.

lord it over OPTIONS: dominate (but see DOMINATE), bully, boss, act superior.

lordly OPTIONS: arrogant, haughty, proud, snobbish, condescending, posh, stately, dignified, well-bred, elegant.

Letters of Address

When you do not know the sex of the person to whom you are writing, there are several ways to address a letter. Never use 'Dear Sir(s)' unless you are certain the addressee(s) is/are male; the person on the receiving end is just as likely to be a woman, and you diminish the effectiveness of your letter if you assume otherwise. 'Dear Madam or Sir' (or 'Dear Sir or Madam') is perhaps the best option for most letters that require some degree of formality. When writing to institutions, such as mail-order companies, it can be appropriate simply to address 'To whom it may concern', or to leave off any salutation, as in a memo, using instead a 'To:' line indicating the name of the company or organisation, and possibly a reference line ('Re:') to lead into your letter.

It is always better, however, to be as specific as possible. To be most effective in terms of making sure your letter reaches the correct person, it is worth taking the time to find out the person's name by making a simple telephone call. You can then use the person's full name, or, if you prefer, the last name preceded by an honorific (Ms, Mr) (see **topic note** on page 39). Use a professional title if you know that the addressee uses one (Dr, Professor). If, as happens in some cases, you know the name but are not sure of the sex, leave off any honorific (Ms, Mr) and use the full name; never assume one way or the other.

If you cannot use the person's name, or you do not have a specific person in mind, use the general job title (Editor, Agent, Manager, Representative). You might also be addressing a certain category or group (Neighbour, Friend, Member).

∗ ∗

M

machismo Although *machismo* has been used to refer to women, this term (and MACHO) is specifically male (from the Spanish for 'male'). There is no parallel female term. Depending on the context, it can be appropriate to replace it with a more specific, gender-neutral term even when referring exclusively to men.
OPTIONS: courage, strength, mettle, bravado, muscle, pride, swagger, self-confidence, over-confidence, aggressiveness, potency.

macho See also MACHISMO.
OPTIONS: courageous, strong, brave, self-confident, over-confident, aggressive, stalwart, pushy, tough, proud, potent.

madam Used for both brothel owners and as an honorific used for women where *sir* would be used for men. Pretentious but convenient in some situations, and probably here to stay. Be sure to use in ways parallel to *sir*.

madman *Madman* and *madwoman* have very different connotations, so *madman* is sometimes used as a generic term where the gender is unknown or unspecified. Often replacing the term is the most clear. Beware also that the term is often used way out of proportion to its context.
OPTIONS: psychopath, lunatic, mad person, wild person, obsessive.

maestro From the Italian for 'master', and usually applied to men only. Like *master*, however, it may be appropriate to use for both women and men (when referring to a conductor, for instance). See MASTER.

maid Do not use to refer to a young girl or to any unmarried woman. See also OLD MAID.
OPTIONS: cleaner, domestic worker, helper, housekeeper, server, janitor.

maiden 1. As a general modifier (meaning 'first', for example), this is a sexist term, relying on the stereotype of the 'untried virgin'. Replace.
OPTIONS: first, premier, debut, new, earliest, initial, inaugural, initiation.
2. As a modifier meaning 'unmarried', this is usually an unnecessary term. If marital status is important (which it usually is not), replace with a less loaded term, but use these carefully – the use of the 'un' prefix can suggest a negative condition.
OPTIONS: unmarried, single, (sometimes) unwed, unattached.

maiden aunt This is a sexist term in that it associates being unmarried with being a virgin, and also with being rejected and 'left on the shelf', both outdated stereotypes. Marital status is rarely relevant in this context. Avoid. See also MAIDEN; SPINSTER.

maidenhead OPTION: hymen.

maiden name OPTIONS: birth name, given name, own name, family name.

maiden speech OPTIONS: first speech, Parliamentary debut, inaugural speech.

maiden voyage OPTIONS: first voyage, first sailing, initiation.

maid of honour OPTIONS: bride's attendant, chief attendant, best woman (parallel to *best man*).

maintenance man OPTIONS: maintenance worker, repair person, caretaker.

male bonding A tired cliché, often used to excuse 'matiness' and 'old boy networks' that exclude women from decision-making and power circles. It was coined in the early 1970s, no doubt as a response to what is now referred to as the 'second wave' of feminism. Be careful how it is used.

male nurse Avoid *male* and *female* as modifiers before job titles. If gender is relevant (which it often is not), include elsewhere in sentence if it is not evident from the context ('Joe Public, a nurse, spends most of his time at the hospital'; 'The percentage of nurses who are men is growing'). See MIDWIFE; ORDERLY.

man Do not use *man* and ' –man' compounds as generic terms to refer to women, mixed-sex groups, or in contexts where the sex is unknown (such as hypothetical scenarios or for general use when a specific person is not being referred to). There are many alternatives; replace unless using specifically for a male person. See topic note on page 62.

man (noun) See topic note on page 62.
1. OPTIONS: person, human, humans, humankind, humanity, people, society, civilisation, we.
2. (games) OPTIONS: piece, person, marker. See also CHESS.

man (verb) 'First manned space flight' could become 'first space flight with humans on board' or 'first crewed space flight'; 'man the lifeboat' could become 'operate/control the lifeboat'; 'man the barri-

cades' could become 'mount the barricades'. See **topic note** on page 62.
OPTIONS: staff, run, handle, operate, crew, use, cover, work, control, steer.

to a man OPTIONS: unanimously, without exception, all people.

man about town OPTIONS: sophisticate, high-flier, social butterfly.

man and wife OPTIONS: husband and wife, partners, man and woman.

manage Not a sexist term. It derives from *manus*, Latin for 'hand'.

manageress Use *manager* for women and men. See **topic note** on page 26.
OPTION: manager.

man-eater An offensive notion as well as term. Avoid. See also FEMME FATALE; LADIES' MAN.

man-eating Often suffers from hysterical over-use, as in 'man-eating black flies'. Be specific, and relate to context.
OPTIONS: human-eating, flesh-eating, blood-sucking, carnivorous, cannibalistic.

mandate Not a sexist term. It derives from *manus*, Latin for 'hand'.

manhandle OPTIONS: handle roughly, mistreat, abuse, strong-arm, subdue, overcome.

manhole OPTIONS: sewer access hole, sewer opening, utility hole, service access, inspection chamber, sewer shaft.

manhood Often used in the gender-neutral sense of strength or responsibility, in which case replace. See also MACHISMO.
OPTIONS: adulthood, mettle, courage.

man-hours OPTIONS: person-hours, work hours, labour hours, time.

manhunt OPTIONS: hunt, search, police search, chase.

manipulate Not a sexist term. It derives from *manus*, Latin for 'hand'.

man in the street, man on the Clapham omnibus OPTIONS: average person/citizen/worker/voter, people in general, person on the street.

man jack, every OPTIONS: every single person, everyone, all.

mankind See topic note on page 62.
OPTIONS: humans, humankind, humanity, civilisation, human beings, human race, people.

manly Be careful how it is used. Not everyone associates the same characteristics with 'being a man', so it is sometimes clearer to replace with a more specific term. See also LADYLIKE; MACHO.
OPTIONS: courageous, brave, strong, aggressive, tough, hard, unfeeling, insensitive, stubborn, virile.

man-made OPTIONS: constructed, artificial, human-caused, human-made, engineered, manufactured, synthetic, simulated.

man manager OPTIONS: personnel manager, human resources professional.

mannequin From the Dutch *mannekin*, a diminutive of 'man'.
OPTIONS: model, display dummy, display figure, dressmaker's dummy.

manning (noun) OPTIONS: staffing, job levels.

manoeuvre Not a sexist term. It derives from *manus*, Latin for 'hand'.

man of God OPTIONS: cleric, member of the clergy, minister, priest, prophet, saint, believer.

man of letters OPTIONS: person of letters, literary person, writer, author, intellectual, scholar, woman of letters/man of letters.

man of science OPTIONS: scientist (or use specific discipline – eg biologist, geneticist), woman of science/man of science.

man of the cloth OPTIONS: cleric, member of the clergy, minister, priest.

man of the house 'If 'head of the household' is what is meant (for example, for market research purposes), replace with a gender-neutral term (although the notion that one family member is responsible for household decision-making does not fit many households). Otherwise, be specific (eg father, husband, male partner).
OPTIONS: householder, head of the house.

man of the people OPTION: populist.

man of the world OPTIONS: worldly person, cosmopolitan type, sophisticate, world traveller, woman of the world/man of the world.

man-of-war 1. Retain for Portuguese man-of-war; there is no suitable alternative that would be commonly understood.
2. OPTIONS: warship, battleship.

manor Not a sexist term. It derives from *manere*, Latin for 'remain'.

man or mouse, Are you a? Avoid this challenge altogether, unless using ironically. If necessary, replace with something more descriptive.
OPTIONS: brave or meek, tough or timid.

man overboard OPTIONS: person overboard, someone overboard, overboard!

manpower The use of this term renders invisible an entire half of the labour force. Replace.
OPTIONS: labour, strength, force, workforce, staff, resources, people, personnel.

man-sized OPTIONS: large, extra large, outsize, hearty, jumbo.

manslaughter Alternatives that could be adopted by the courts include *humanslaughter* and *murder without malice*. As long as this is a specific legal charge (as distinct from murder), however, it cannot be substituted in that context. In other contexts, replace.
OPTIONS: murder, killing, slaying, homicide, assassination, execution.

man's inhumanity to man OPTIONS: inhumanity, cruelty, one's inhumanity to another.

man to man OPTIONS: person to person, face to face.

Manxman This usage demonstrates that compounds with ' –man' are not gender-neutral – consider the absurd sound of 'She's a Manxman'. Replacing such terms can require reconstructing the sentence – such as by changing 'She's/He's a Manxman' to 'She's/He's Manx' or 'She's/He's from the Isle of Man'. For plural usage, 'the Manx' is better than 'Manxmen'. See topic note on page 63.
OPTIONS: Manxman/Manxwoman, Manx, person from Isle of Man.

marketing man OPTIONS: marketer, market researcher, advertiser, market executive, copywriter.

marksman OPTIONS: sharpshooter, sniper, shooter, markswoman/marksman, shot.

master The word derives from the Latin *magister*, meaning 'master' or 'chief'. It could be argued that its relation to *magis* ('more') and *magnus* ('big') (and thus to English words like *magistrate*, *magnitude*, and *magisterial*) make it non-sexist; indeed most people have no objections to the word and to its compounds. Some do object to it and its widespread use in so-called gender-neutral words and compounds, especially considering that its female 'counterpart', MISTRESS, is almost exclusively reduced to its sexual use. Compounds with ' –mistress' are now coloured by this meaning, even ones in common use: *headmistress*, *postmistress*. Both of these are easily replaced in most circumstances.

Master is rarely used in full as a courtesy title; for adult males, it has been replaced by *Mr* (the abbreviation of *Mister*), and for boys it is outdated (see **topic note** on page 39).

Some official titles (Master of the Rolls, Master of the Queen's Music) must be kept as is.

master (noun) Not always considered sexist (see MASTER main entry), so can be used for both women and men or replaced with a gender-neutral term. See also DOMINATE.
OPTIONS: head, leader, principal, chief, expert, owner, controller, proprietor, governor, judge.

master (verb) Not always considered sexist (see MASTER main entry), so can be used for both women and men or replaced with a gender-neutral term. See also DOMINATE.
1. OPTIONS: beat, conquer, subjugate, control, dominate, rule, command.
2. OPTIONS: achieve, excel at, grasp, become proficient in, gain command of, handle.

master (adj) OPTIONS: expert, skilled, gifted, accomplished, chief, leading, foremost, dominant, first, primary, paramount, main, top, pre-eminent, predominant, arch, prevailing, supreme.

master bedroom OPTIONS: main bedroom, largest bedroom.

master of ceremonies Using the abbreviated form, MC, is often acceptable for women or men.
OPTIONS: MC, presenter, host, leader of ceremonies.

master class OPTIONS: virtuoso class, expert tutorial.

master copy OPTIONS: original, top copy, first copy.

master key OPTIONS: pass key, original key.

mastermind (noun) OPTIONS: genius, virtuoso, ace, sage, inventor, originator, leader, director, commander, engineer.

mastermind (verb) OPTIONS: direct, plan, command, guide, coordinate, engineer, invent, originate, develop.

master of one's fate OPTIONS: controller/director/commander of one's fate, in control, at the reins.

masterpiece OPTIONS: great work, classic, achievement, greatest work, *tour de force*, work of art, museum piece, brainchild, *chef-d'œuvre*.

master's degree Using the abbreviated form is often acceptable. See also BACHELOR'S DEGREE.
OPTIONS: MA, graduate degree, advanced degree.

mastery OPTIONS: command, control, skill, understanding, grasp, proficiency, grip, conquest.

mate Often used as a form of address to perpetuate an 'old boys network', a male alliance that excludes women, especially from decision-making circles. It has long been used for either sex, however, but it retains a strong association with male-only groups and what is referred to as 'male bonding'. Be careful how it is used.

maternal instinct OPTIONS: parental instinct, nurturing instinct.

matrimonial See MATRIMONY.
OPTIONS: marital, conjugal, wedded.

matrimony The male 'equivalent', *patrimony*, has a very different meaning. When *matrimony* began to be used for the state of being married, inheritance was most likely always through the father, thus *patrimony* (deriving from *pater*, Latin for 'father'). Being married, and bearing children, was woman's 'inheritance'. Today, both terms have sexist implications and are outdated. The Anglican Alternative Service Book (1980) uses 'The Marriage Service' instead of *matrimony*; the Catholic New Marriage Book (1975) uses 'the Rite of Marriage during Mass' (*The Observer*, 22 November 1992). See also NUPTIAL.
OPTIONS: marriage, marriage service, marriage rites, wedlock, union.

matron An example of unparallel usage; the male 'counterpart', *patron*, has a very different meaning and is used inclusively for women and men (but see PATRON). From the Latin for 'mother', *matron* used to refer to any married, settled woman (as opposed to *maid*). Hence *matron* is, according to *Collins' English Dictionary*,

'associated with a middle-aged, usually plump, woman'. Today, it is more often used as a job title (or as a modifier; see MATRONLY), in which case it should be replaced.
OPTIONS: superintendent, head, chief, manager, director, principal officer, nursing officer, warden.

matronly Replace with a more specific term that is used for both women and men. See also MATRON.
OPTIONS: staid, dignified, mature, middle-aged, sedate, established.

matron of honour There is no need to distinguish between married and unmarried attendants. Replace. See also MAID OF HONOUR.
OPTIONS: bride's attendant, chief attendant, best woman (parallel to *best man*).

Mayor A sexist tradition gives us one of the most absurd titles for public office: Mr Mayor, for male or female. Women mayors were saved being labelled 'mayoress' because that was reserved for the wives of mayors. 'Lady mayor' and 'consort' were reserved for the relatives accompanying the mayor. Drop the Mr, leave the Mayor.

medicine man Specific to Native Americans, among others, but now often used in a derogatory way. Avoid.
OPTIONS: healer, shaman, natural doctor, homeopathic healer/doctor, homeopathist, herbalist.

men Use context-specific alternatives, such as in military usage. See topic note on page 62.
OPTIONS: troops, soldiers, operators, players, pieces (as in games).

men from boys (to separate) OPTIONS: experienced from inexperienced, old from young, strong from weak.

men of violence OPTIONS: terrorists, bombers, men and women of violence, people of violence.

mermaid An example of unparallel usage; its male 'equivalent' is *merman*.
OPTIONS: merwoman/merman, sea goddess/sea god, sea creature, sea nymph, spirit of the sea.

meter maid OPTIONS: parking warden, meter attendant.

middleman OPTIONS: intermediary, go-between, middleperson.

midwife The term derives from the Old English *mid*, for 'with', and *wif*, for 'woman'; some writers believe 'woman' here refers to the woman giving birth, not the helper – making it a non-sexist term

(Maggio, 1988). Generally, however, the term is understood to have originally referred to a woman by whose means a delivery is effected. It is used in an inclusive sense for both men and women, but (like *nurse*, also considered a female profession) it is sometimes wrongly preceded by 'male'. Because of this (and because most dictionaries continue to define it as 'a woman . . .'), some might consider it sexist and want to replace it with *birth attendant*. Retain as an official job title, however.

1. OPTION: birth attendant.
2. (general noun) OPTIONS: instrument, facilitator, agent.
3. (verb) OPTIONS: bring forth, assist, bring about, facilitate.

milkmaid OPTION: milker.

milkman OPTION: milk deliverer.

miss Like its counterpart 'sir', this is an outmoded usage. On the school playground, it could be replaced with actual surnames, preceded by *Ms* or *Mr* where appropriate, or with first names.
As an honorific, *Ms* is far more useful and should be used where *Mr* would be used, except where a woman has expressed a preference to be addressed as *Miss*. See MS; topic note on page 39.

mistress 1. In the sexual context, there is no male parallel. Although terms like 'toyboy', 'gigolo', 'bimboy' and 'bit of rough' are used, none has the same 'acceptability' as *mistress*, and none applies specifically to the lover of a married woman. There are, however, many terms for the lover of a married man; we tend to label the women in such relationships but not the men (*mistress, kept woman, other woman*). Replace in this context with a less judgemental term that is used for both women and men.
OPTIONS: lover, girlfriend/boyfriend, paramour (though this can be used derogatorily).
2. Replace in compounds. See HEADMISTRESS; POSTMISTRESS; SCHOOLMISTRESS.
3. Because of its association with 'loose' sexuality, *mistress* is rarely used nowadays in other contexts, as a female 'equivalent' of *master*. The sexual connotations now colour it, making it a non-parallel term. Replace.
OPTIONS: head (of household), homemaker, main shopper/consumer; leader, principal, chief, owner, proprietor, director, controller, governor, judge, expert. For someone who is proficient at a skill or talent, consider using MASTER or MAESTRO.
4. Retain in official titles: Mistress of the Robes.

modern man OPTIONS: modern society, contemporary society, people today, homo sapiens.

moneymen OPTIONS: funders, backers, financers, sponsors, producers, benefactors, donors, patrons (but see PATRON).

mother (noun) 1. Use strictly in the sense of 'female parent' or for a senior member of a religious order (mother superior). Do not use as a generic term for 'parent'; it reinforces stereotypes of parenting roles that are sexist and outdated (see specific examples below).
2. Replace when used in the sense of 'begetter' or 'founder', even if the subject is female. The terms *mother* and *father* have very different connotations and so are not used in a balanced, parallel way in this context. Note the discrepancy between, for example, 'Curie is the mother of radioactivity' and 'Faraday is the father of electricity'.
OPTIONS: founder, begetter, creator, originator, source, inventor.
3. Do not use as a general modifier (see specific examples below).
OPTIONS: first, model, primary, main, source, ultimate; natural, innate, native.

mother (verb) 'To mother' has a very different meaning from 'to father'; according to *Collins' English Dictionary*, it means 'to give birth to or produce; to nurture, protect, etc.' as opposed to 'to beget; to create, found, originate, etc.' Yet both mothers and fathers are capable of doing what is characterised as 'mothering'. Be careful not to use the term in a way that promotes sexist and outdated stereotypes of parenting roles. See also FATHER (verb).
OPTIONS: nurture, care for, suckle, attend to, protect, support, foster.

mother and baby room OPTIONS: changing/feeding room, child care room, baby changing area.

mother and toddler groups OPTIONS: toddler playgroups, parent and toddler groups, parent-supervised playgroups.

motherboard Has a specific meaning in electronics and should be retained in this context (although alternatives that could be adopted by the computer industry include *parentboard* and *primary circuit board*).

mother cell Has a specific scientific meaning (relating to cell reproduction) that should be retained.

mother country OPTIONS: native land/country, homeland, birthplace, country of origin.

mother courage OPTION: courage.

Mother Earth OPTION: earth or Earth.

motherland OPTIONS: home country, native land, homeland, homeground, the old country, birthplace.

Mother Nature OPTION: nature or Nature.

mother of all battles OPTIONS: ultimate battle, most impressive battle.

mother of the chapel OPTIONS: shop steward, union leader, representative, foreworker, mother of the chapel/father of the chapel.

mother of parliaments Sexist and inaccurate jingoism. If you must use, try *the Westminster model* or *model parliament*. Otherwise, be specific: British Parliament or Westminster.

mother-of-pearl Usually best to leave as is.
OPTIONS: nacre, nacreous.

mothers Often used instead of *parents*, in which case use that word.

mother's helper OPTIONS: babysitter, nanny, housekeeper, cleaner, cook, handyperson, parents' helper, au pair.

mother ship OPTION: supply ship.

mother tongue OPTIONS: native language, native tongue, first language, native speech, vernacular.

MPs and their wives Be careful of this usage, which has the effect of making all female MPs invisible. If it is necessary to use this construction, replace with 'MPs and their spouses' or 'MPs and their husbands and wives'.

Mrs *Ms* is far more useful as an honorific and should be used where *Mr* would be used, except where a woman has expressed a preference to be addressed as *Mrs*. See MS; topic note on page 39.

Ms This is the most appropriate courtesy title for any woman, whatever her marital status. It effectively makes obsolete the formerly used titles *Miss* and *Mrs*. Although listed as an option on most forms, it has not in practice replaced *Miss* and *Mrs* and is not accepted universally. Generally, use the term for all women where you would use *Mr* for men; do not use where no titles are used or where a professional title (such as Dr) is used. Some women may express a preference for being addressed as *Miss* or *Mrs*, in such cases use the preferred form. If marital status is not known, opt for *Ms*. Plural is *Mses*. or *Mss*. See topic note on page 39.

mum Do not use as a generic term for 'parent'. See MOTHER.

mum's the word Not a sexist phrase. *Mum* in this sense comes from a request for silence, originating in the fourteenth century, and suggests the act of closing one's lips.

mummy Not a sexist term; in its sense of 'preserved body', it derives from the Persian for 'wax'.

Mum's Army A sexist term to describe untrained teachers' assistants (most often parents). The government recently suggested putting them to greater use as teachers for younger children (who, it was thought, do not require professionally trained teachers), but backed down after an outcry from teachers' groups.

OPTIONS: teachers' assistants, classroom assistants, parent helpers.

* * * * * * * * * * * TOPIC NOTE * * * * * * * * * * *

Man and Mankind

Man and *mankind* are sometimes referred to as 'pseudogenerics': they are used as generic terms, intended to include both men and women, but they are inherently masculine and are understood to be masculine. 'Man' used in this way is ambiguous: 'The Australopithecus must have been a man', for example, sounds as if it means that the Australopithecus must have been male. The full sentence, however, reads 'The Australopithecus must have been a man because man is the only animal that can invent', suggesting that 'man' actually means 'human'.

Using man and mankind generically is ineffective, offensive, and unnecessary. There are many alternative terms that can be used to say what you mean far more clearly:

humans, humankind, human race, human species, humanity, human nature, people, persons, folk, public, citizens, citizenry, population, society, civilisation, community, world, everyone, anyone, you and me, we, us, earthlings, mortals, warm-blooded creatures, flesh and blood, participants, workers, voters, inhabitants, residents

Avoiding the use of *man* as a generic term gives us the opportunity of retrieving its original meaning of 'male' – useful when a sign saying 'Men's toilet' means just that.

* * * * * * * * * * * **TOPIC NOTE** * * * * * * * * * * * *

' –man' Words

One of the most compelling and clearly illustratable reasons for eliminating sexist language is that it does not suit the way we live now. Compound words using –man are good examples of this.

Job titles and descriptions are one category of –man compounds. *Craftsman*, *milkman* and *foreman* may once have been used to describe occupations held exclusively by men. Today, however, they are just as likely to refer to women as to men. Replacing these gender-based job titles ensures that you avoid ambiguity. Does the sentence 'The average salesman for the company earns up to £15,000 per year', for example, include the women who sell for the company? It is unclear the way the sentence is written. By saying 'The average salesperson (or sales representative) earns. . .', you can avoid any possible misunderstandings. (This also then frees the word *salesman* for its intended use – to apply to men only. It is likely, for example, that, through job discrimination, the company's average sales*man* referred to above earns more than its average sales*woman*, though both are in the same job.)

The fact that there have long been words ending in –woman – *charwoman*, *washerwoman*, *gentlewoman* – indicates that it cannot be assumed that words ending in –man include women. Otherwise, there would have been no need for these words – *charman*, *washerman* and *gentleman* would have been used as the 'generic' terms, which they clearly are not (Miller and Swift, 1989: 33).

63

Similarly with other –man compounds. Most –man and –men compounds do sound male to us; research has shown that people, especially young people, interpret words using –man as masculine. If they were truly meant to include women as well as men, the following sentence, which appeared in the *Irish Times*, would not sound as absurd as it does: 'The annual rate of Irishmen travelling for that purpose [to have abortions] is higher now than in 1983 (*Guardian*, 1 April 1992).

One way to deal with these 'false generics' is to use –man and –woman compounds in sex-specific ways (or together when the sex of the subjects is not known). Many –man compounds have acceptable –woman parallels; the above sentence, for example, should have read 'The annual rate of Irishwomen. . .'. Others with a long history include *spokeswoman* and *saleswoman*. When retaining –man words and using them in conjunction with –woman words ('The craftswomen and craftsmen displayed their work'), be sure to use them in a balanced way. Do not, for example, use 'craftsmen and women'.

Another option is to replace the –man with –person (eg *spokesperson*). Although this is an acceptable, clear, and easy alternative, it has been the butt of many jokes about political correctness and so has not enjoyed much success (see **topic notes** on CHAIRMAN on page 19; **notes** on POLITICAL CORRECTNESS in Introduction).

Yet another option for replacing false generics is to use an alternative, gender-neutral term that can be applied to men and women (*artisan* for example, rather than *craftsman*). This is true of most –man compounds: a different word altogether can be the best option, eliminating sexism and enhancing clarity by being more specific. In many cases, this is easiest done by replacing –man at the end of the word with –er: a fisher fishes, for example, much as a hunter hunts or a teacher teaches. The individual entries in this book offer alternatives of this type.

Terms denoting nationality or origin (Frenchman, Dutchman) can present unique problems and need to be dealt with as individual cases. They are ambiguous as often used. The saying 'An Englishman's home is his castle', for instance, in some contexts is meant to refer to men only, as in 'a man is king at home and rules the roost'. In other contexts, it is meant to refer to women and men, as in 'the English are proud home owners'. Some of these terms have several suitable alternatives: Scot, for instance, instead of Scotsman. Others do not: Cornishman, for instance, can be replaced by the more awkward 'person from Cornwall'. New forms can be generated to solve this problem (Ulsterer for Ulsterman, for instance), but it will take some time before they catch on widely. In the meantime, if using both –man and –woman compounds, remember to use them in a parallel way, as described above.

Sometimes *man* or *men* appears within a word that is not sexist. This is because some words with 'man' – such as *manager* and *manipulate* – derive from the Latin *manus* (hand). The words *woman* and *human*, similarly, are not sexist (see WOMAN). Some words that include *man* and are frequently mistaken as sexist are included in the dictionary section.

* *

N

nag (noun) OPTIONS: pest, nuisance.

nag (verb) Avoid using in a way that reinforces negative stereotypes of women. In such contexts, replace with a less loaded term that can be applied equally to women and men. See also BITCH, DOMINATE, PUSSY-WHIPPED, SCOLD, SHREW.
OPTIONS: pester, harass, irritate, browbeat, hound, bully, push, plague, demand, gripe.

nanny (noun) Because it has no male parallel, this term (like AU PAIR) should be used for both female and male professional nannies. In reality, however, most nannies are female, and if the feminine sound is objected to, replace with a more general term. (Be aware, however, that *nanny* is the term used by professionals and agencies; like *au pair*, it describes specific duties and responsibilities not synonymous with many of the alternatives.)
OPTIONS: babysitter, childminder, caregiver, nurse.

nanny (verb) OPTIONS: hand hold, be overprotective, patronise.

nanny state OPTIONS: welfare state, bureaucracy.

Neanderthal man OPTIONS: Neanderthal human, a Neanderthal, early human.

née From the French 'to be born', this is similar in meaning to 'birth name' (see MAIDEN NAME). Not necessarily sexist, although the practice that leads to it (ie women taking their husband's name at marriage) is.

Negress Sexist and racist (avoid *Negro* as well).
OPTIONS: black woman, Black, woman/person of colour.

new man Suggests that being caring or sensitive are 'new' and unusual characteristics for a man; frequently it is used ironically. Recently, pollsters have adopted *newish man* after finding a dearth of new men available. Avoid both, except when using ironically (in which case place in quotation marks). See NEW WOMAN.

newsboy/newsgirl BOY and GIRL, even if used in a balanced and sex-specific way, can be offensive because they are often applied to people of any age, especially to those who hold service jobs. Better to replace with a gender-neutral term.

OPTIONS: newspaper deliverer, newspaper seller/vendor, newspaper carrier.

newsman OPTIONS: reporter, journalist, newsreader, news anchor, anchorperson, newspaper owner, media representative.

newspaperman See NEWSMAN.

new woman Suggests that being independent, assertive, or self-sufficient are characteristics that are 'new' or unusual for a woman. Avoid. See NEW MAN.

night watchman OPTIONS: night guard, watch, security guard, attendant.

nobleman/noblewoman OPTIONS: noble, nobleperson, member of the nobility, peer, aristocrat, nobleman/noblewoman. Another option is to use specific titles, such as duchess/duke, lady/lord.

no man's land OPTIONS: unclaimed territory, wilderness, unchartered land, uninhabited land, unpeopled area, wasteland, limbo land, no-go area, dead zone, free-fire zone, demilitarised zone, grey area, vacuum.

Norseman This usage demonstrates that compounds with ' –man' are not gender-neutral – consider the absurd sound of 'She's a Norseman'. Replacing such terms can require reconstructing the sentence – such as 'She's/He's a Norseman' to 'She's/He's Norse'. For plural usage, 'the Norse' is better than 'Norsemen'. See **topic note** on page 63.
OPTIONS: Viking, Norse, Norwegian, (plural) the Norse.

nuptial This word derives from the Latin *nubere*, meaning 'to cover oneself for the bridegroom'. It has moved far enough away from its original meaning, however, to be considered non-sexist. See MATRIMONY; PRENUPTIAL AGREEMENT.
OPTIONS: marriage, wedding, conjugal, mating.

nurse Use for both female and male, and never precede with 'male'. See MALE NURSE; ORDERLY; SISTER.

nurseryman OPTIONS: nursery worker, gardener.

nymphet The concept behind this term (as with LOLITA) is itself offensive. A young woman who is sexually active is simply that; a very young woman (or girl) who is considered desirable or even flirtatious should not be labelled. Instead, label the man (usually older) who harbours sexual thoughts about young girls. See LOLITA; NYMPHOMANIA.

nymphomania Defined by *Collins' English Dictionary* as 'a neurotic condition in women' who are compelled to have sex with as many men as possible, *nymphomania* has a male 'counterpart', *satyriasis* – a term that is rarely heard. *Nymphomaniac* is often used casually to describe any woman considered sexually available or indiscriminate; the parallel terms for men (*lothario, ladies' man, womaniser*) are much less scathing. Use the term cautiously, or replace wth a gender-neutral term that can equally apply to women and men. OPTIONS: promiscuous, sexually active.

O

oarsman OPTIONS: rower, boat-handler, paddler, sculler, punter, boater.

office girl OPTIONS: office assistant, office junior.

the Old Lady of Threadneedle Street OPTION: Bank of England.

old maid 1. Do not use for an unmarried mature woman. See SPINSTER.
2. Do not use as a modifier for women and men ('old maidish').
OPTIONS: fussy, fusspot, prim, lonely, repressed, fastidious.
3. Although it is the official name of a well-known card game, it is also known as Pass the Lady and Old Boy (from the French *Le Vieux Garçon*). It could also be referred to as Odd One Out.

Old Master Because of its use of MASTER, this term is considered sexist by some. Also, it implies that there is a canon of European artworks and artists which everyone agrees is a model of classic painting. Better to be specific, using artists' names or painting styles. See also MASTERPIECE.
OPTIONS: classic artist, great artist; classic work.

old wives' tale Some writers suggest using this term in a positive sense to describe the invaluable knowledge and wisdom passed down through generations by women (Miller and Swift, 1989: 146). If using in its original sense, replace with a gender-neutral term, and be sensitive to whether you intend a positive or negative connotation.
OPTIONS: popular folklore, ancestral wisdom, common knowledge, folktale, superstitious story, myth, legend, misconception.

old woman As an insult, most often directed towards men, this is offensive to women and pensioners.
OPTIONS: fusspot, fusser, fuddy-duddy, goody-goody.

ombudsman From the Swedish for 'administration man'. Difficult to replace as an official title, although 'ombudsperson' is used to some extent in the US, and 'ombudsman/ombudswoman' used in gender-specific ways are acceptable.
OPTIONS: ombudsperson, ombudsman/ombudswoman, ombud, complaints investigator.

one man one vote OPTIONS: one person one vote, universal suffrage.

one-man show OPTIONS: one-person show, single-artist exhibit, solo performance.

oneupmanship OPTIONS: competition, rivalry, one-upping.

orderly Used for men only in the health care context. Replace with a gender-neutral term used for both women and men. See MALE NURSE; NURSE; SISTER.
OPTIONS: nursing assistant, hospital attendant.

P

Page Three girl The 'tradition' of featuring nude or seminude women in widely read newspapers may be on its way out, according to Rupert Murdoch, whose newspaper started it. Nevertheless, the term has now become a generic (meaning pin-up); while the concept is with us, at least remove 'girl' from the term. See GIRL.
OPTIONS: Page Three model, pin-up, topless model.

paper boy OPTIONS: paper seller, newspaper deliverer.

pater/patria Words derived from the Latin for 'father' and 'fatherland' are considered sexist by many people, although many of the terms are used in inclusive senses – *patriot, patron, patronising*. Alternatives are provided with selected individual terms for those who want to replace them.

paternal Use only when referring to 'father' or 'fatherly' (as in *paternal grandparent*).
OPTIONS: parental, nurturing, protective.

paternalism Derives from the Latin for 'father', the root of many English words. Although it is used mostly in an inclusive sense now, its meaning relies on an outdated and sexist stereotype of father-like authority. Because of this, some people object to its use except when referring to domination or authority that is specifically male.
OPTIONS: authoritarianism, political intervention, domination (but see DOMINATE), protectionism, parentalism, 'benevolent' despotism.

patriarch Use only for male figure; otherwise, replace.
OPTIONS: head of family, elder, ancestor.

patrician OPTIONS: noble, aristocratic, genteel, blue-blooded.

patrimony The female 'equivalent', MATRIMONY, has a completely different meaning.
OPTIONS: inheritance, birthright, legacy, estate, succession, heritage, endowment.

patriot/patriotic Derives from the Latin for 'fatherland', but used in an inclusive sense. Because of its roots, however, some object to its use in non-sex-specific contexts. See also PATRIOTISM.
OPTIONS: nationalist, jingoist, loyalist, good citizen, civic-minded.

patriotism See PATRIOT/PATRIOTIC.
OPTIONS: nationalism, love of one's country, jingoism, good citizenship, allegiance.

patrolman OPTIONS: patroller, patrol, guard, watch, lookout, sentinel, sentry, scout, traffic/motorway officer, warden.

patron Although it is used inclusively for women and men, the term derives from the Latin for 'father', and its feminine 'counterpart', MATRON, has very different meanings. Because of this, some people consider it to be sexist.
OPTIONS: benefactor, financer, backer, donor, sponsor, protector, guardian.

patronage See PATRON.
1. OPTIONS: custom, trade, business.
2. OPTIONS: support, fosterage, protection, sponsorship, favouritism, nepotism.

patroness See topic note on page 26.
OPTION: patron.

patronising See PATRON.
OPTIONS: condescending, acting superior, haughty, arrogant.

patron saint OPTION: guardian saint.

paymaster Because of its incorporation of the word *master*, some consider this sexist. See MASTER.
OPTIONS: treasurer, financial officer, accountant, bursar, purser, bookkeeper, wage payer, controller, cashier.

peeping Tom Based on a legendary male character (a tailor who peeked at the naked Lady Godiva), so it could be retained on the grounds of historical accuracy. It does imply a male subject, however, so when used in a gender-neutral sense, replace.
OPTIONS: peeper, voyeur, eavesdropper.

peeress Use *peer* to refer to a woman who is a peer in her own right. Otherwise, the wife or widow of a peer should be referred to by her own name or as Lady So-and-So.

penmanship OPTIONS: handwriting, longhand, script, writing, hand.

–person As a suffix (or sometimes prefix) fixed to –man words, this has been the butt of many jokes about political correctness (*personhole*, *personslaughter*), but it has its uses. 'Chairperson', for example, is perfectly acceptable, though it is objected to by many and is often used only when referring to women, retaining 'chairman' for men. Often, a better word can be found: *chair, sewer access,* etc. Specific entries list a ' –person' option as a non-sexist alternative where one is available and in common use (eg *spokesperson*). See also topic note on ' –man' words.

philanderer The term could be applied equally to men and women (it is from the Greek for 'lover of men' and originally may have referred to homosexual lovers), but in reality it is most often applied to men and is defined by many dictionaries as 'one who flirts with women'. Like WOMANISER and LADIES' MAN, it does not have negative connotations; the female 'equivalents', however, tend to be derogatory and offensive: *slut, whore, mistress.* Use *philanderer* in a balanced way for men and women, or replace.
OPTIONS: heartbreaker, indiscriminate lover, flirt, seducer.

Pilgrim Fathers OPTION: Pilgrims.

pin money This was historically the allowance paid by a husband to a wife for managing the household and personal expenses (including, literally, pins). Its sexist connotations continued with its more recent sense of money for trivial or incidental expenses (basically, the unimportant things that women spend money on).
OPTIONS: petty cash, household money, spending money, splurge money, mad money.

pitman OPTIONS: miner, coal miner, pit worker.

placeman OPTIONS: appointee, functionary, bureaucrat, agent.

plain man's guide OPTIONS: plain person's guide, everyone's guide, layperson's guide.

plainsman OPTIONS: plains dweller, plainswoman/plainsman.

ploughman's lunch Generally best to retain since it is a commonly used term and is found on pub menus, but experiment with alternatives, including 'plougher's lunch'.
OPTIONS: plougher's lunch, cheese and pickle plate, ploughperson's lunch.

poetess A group of leading British female poets supposedly wish to be referred to as *poettes*, seeking to distinguish themselves from the masses of what they see as second-rate poets. Generally, however, use *poet*.

policeman As a job title, use for male officers only, if also using

policewoman. Where the gender is not known or not specified, replace.
OPTIONS: police constable, police officer, bobby, peace officer, policewoman/policeman.

policeman of the world As a general term (as in 'The UN is the policeman of the world'), replace.
OPTIONS: watchdog, law enforcer, guardian of international law.

politically correct A derogatory label often applied to attempts to reform language use so that it is inclusive and unbiased. For serious use, replace with a more specific term. See page 4 of Introduction.
OPTIONS: inclusive, non-sexist, non-racist, unbiased, non-discriminatory.

postman Royal Mail use *postman* and *postwoman*, or more specific titles such as *delivery staff* or *sorting staff*. Do not use *postie* – postal workers themselves hate it. See topic note on page 78.
OPTIONS: post carrier, letter carrier, post deliverer, postman/postwoman.

postmaster/postmistress Although *postmaster* is one of the few –master compound words used gender specifically, its 'counterpart', *postmistress*, suffers from the illicit and sexual connotations of MISTRESS as used today. See MASTER.
OPTIONS: sub-post office manager, post office manager, postal clerk.

postmaster general Official title which in most cases will need to be retained to prevent misunderstandings. For general use, replace.
OPTIONS: postal chief, federal postal director.

PR man OPTIONS: PR executive, spokesperson, representative.

preceptress See topic note on page 26.
OPTION: precept.

prehistoric man *Prehistoric* is ambiguous as well as sexist (it can refer to any of a number of distinct time periods). In most cases it is better to use a more specific term; otherwise replace with a gender-neutral alternative.
OPTIONS: cave dweller, troglodyte, Neanderthal, prehistoric person, missing link.

prenuptial agreement Because of its incorporation of NUPTIAL (Latin for 'to cover oneself for the bridegroom'), this term could be considered sexist. It has moved far enough away from its original meaning, however, to be considered non-sexist.
OPTIONS: pre-wedding agreement, pre-marriage contract.

pressman OPTIONS: journalist, reporter, news hound, newspaper owner, printer, press operator.

priest Use for male or female.

priestess Do not use for contemporary female priests. Retain only in those historical/cultural contexts in which priestesses played a distinct – and positive – role. See **topic note** on page 26.
OPTION: priest.

prima donna From the Italian for 'first lady', but often used inclusively for men and women.
OPTIONS: lead, principal singer, principal performer, opera star; temperamental person, spoiled brat.

prince Use only in its literal sense for specific male royal. As a general term (meaning 'good person'), replace with a gender-neutral term. See PRINCELY; PRINCESS.
OPTIONS: angel, saint, diamond, salt of the earth, paragon, magnanimous person.

princely As a general modifier, replace. See PRINCE.
OPTIONS: generous, lavish, liberal, magnanimous, sumptuous.

princess Use only in its literal sense for a specific female royal. As a general term, it has very different meanings from those of PRINCE/ PRINCELY, and usually refers to a person considered extremely sweet or snobbish.
OPTIONS: sweetheart, kind person; aristocrat, dignitary; snob, fussy person, spoiled brat.

princess dress OPTIONS: flared dress, waistless dress.

prodigal son OPTIONS: prodigal, wastrel, squanderer, spendthrift; returnee, lost lamb (returning to the fold).

pronouns *He* does not stand for 'he or she', any more than *she* does. Avoid this 'generic' use of 'he'. For specific guidelines, see **topic note** on pronouns on page 79.

prophetess See **topic note** on page 26.
OPTION: prophet.

proprietess See also LANDLORD.
OPTIONS: proprietor, owner, manager, freeholder.

prostitute This gender-neutral term should be used equally with men and with women; it is not necessary to precede it with 'male'. It is free of the judgemental and derogatory overtones of many terms used exclusively for female prostitutes – CALL GIRL, WHORE, SLUT. Also, it avoids the euphemistic tone of FALLEN WOMAN and *woman of the night/streets*. In general avoid these; it is better to use the term that is least likely to be misunderstood. Note also that most terms used to describe the service provider (as listed above) are derogatory, vulgar, or unduly euphemistic. Those few terms used to describe the service buyer (including PUNTER) are relatively mild and nonjudgemental. See **topic note** on page 94.

protegé/protegée Use *protegé* for women and men.

Pullman car Not a sexist term; it derives from the name of its inventor, George M. Pullman, a nineteenth-century American designer.

punter Use for male and female alike. Note, however, that it is also an example of the very mild and nonjudgemental language used to describe men who use the services of prostitutes. As with MISTRESS and LOLITA, we too often label the woman, but not the man, involved in an adulterous or otherwise questionable relationship.

purse strings Not really a sexist term; historically men as well as women carried purses.

pussy-whipped A vulgar contemporary term for 'henpecked', and one that invariably is applied to men seen to be 'nagged' by women. Replace with a term that can be applied equally to women and men. See also DOMINATE; NAG; SCOLD.
OPTIONS: nagged, browbeaten, downtrodden, dominated, bullied, hounded, pestered, harassed, pushed.

* * * * * * * * * * * * TOPIC NOTE * * * * * * * * * * * *

The Police

The Metropolitan Police have had a policy on the use of gender-neutral job titles since 1991, when a special commission recommended doing away with the W prefix on abbreviated titles, such as PC (police constable), PS (police sergeant) and PI (police inspector). Yet WPC is still commonly used by the press, and not just by the tabloids. Furthermore, many women officers wanted to retain the prefix; according to the equal opportunities officers of the Met, and the spokesperson for the Police Federation, there was a 'backlash' by female officers who felt the W prefix was crucial to public awareness of the presence of women among the police ranks. This is perhaps a response to the sexism historically entrenched in the police, both internally and in how they have been perceived by the public. It is clear that eliminating sexist language among the police will not do away with the sexual harassment and discrimination experienced by many female officers. Nevertheless, language reinforces and is reinforced by behaviour, and language's influence on public opinion and on morale among the forces makes it essential that the issue of sexism in the way the police communicate is thoughtfully addressed.

Dismissing the option of using 'he/him/his' to encompass male and female, the police's *Guidelines for the Use of Descriptive Language* tries to rectify the awkwardness of using *he/she* or *s/he* by advising writers to use specific terms where possible: *officer, constable, victim*. This is perhaps the easiest solution to any problem with sexist language, and the most accurate – it not only removes the sexism, but it is less awkward.

In 1992, the Met published *Focusing on Fair Treatment for All*, an equal opportunities handbook for police officers giving information and advice on combatting destructive stereotypes. Among the stereotypes targeted are those of black ycuths as dangerous criminals and Irish people as IRA members/ supporters. It also targets racism, sexism, homophobia and discrimination against the disabled. One aspect of its advice on sexist language involves name-calling of female colleagues 'in derogatory terms, for example Doris and Plonk', and it asks, 'What is the effect of constantly referring to female police officers as girls but to male officers as men?'

In spite of these efforts, the majority of the press has yet to change its use of WPC. Much worse, women officers are often described in terms of appearance – with adjectives like 'young', 'attractive', 'blonde', 'petite', 'big-boned' accompanying their names. One difficulty is that female officers are only beginning to take on the same tasks as their male colleagues.

This is directly related to sexist language because it encourages a view of female police officers as less competent and less able to handle dangerous work than their male colleagues.

* * * * * * * * * * * * TOPIC NOTE * * * * * * * * * * * *

The Post Office

Postal workers have made efforts to combat sexist language in guidelines issued some time ago. Although no generic term has been developed to describe those who deliver the post to households around the country, *postman* and *postwoman* are the terms of choice. This requires, of course, knowing the gender of the postal worker. The term *post carrier* is modelled on *mail carrier*, which has been successfully adopted in the US. The term *postie*, though it has its followers among the popular press, is out of favour within the post office and its use is not encouraged by staff or anyone else.

Internally, Royal Mail opts for specific titles relating to job duty: delivery staff, sorting staff. A letter sent by the personnel department to all department heads in 1987 states that 'Constant use of male terms can cause offence to some women because it could be taken to imply that female employees of the Post Office do not have a place (or command respect) in the Business.' Although the staff letter says there is no need for 'radical change, rather a willingness to look at the matter from a wider viewpoint,' it calls on all staff to incorporate non-sexist language in any revised or new documents.

* * * * * * * * * * * * TOPIC NOTE * * * * * * * * * * * *

Pronouns

The Problem

Using *he* as a generic pronoun – one that is meant to include women as well as men – is outdated and impractical. Nevertheless, it is thought to be firmly rooted in rules of English grammar, and is certainly rooted in custom and practice, so it has long been thought that *he* includes *she*.

This is clearly no longer the case. Research has shown that people (especially children) interpret *he*, *him* and *his* as masculine. Even writers who claim to believe that *he* is truly generic reveal that this is not so when referring to specifically female functions or behaviours. One writer is quoted as saying in an anthropological context: 'As for man, he is no different from the rest. His back aches, he ruptures easily, his women have difficulties in childbirth' (Miller and Swift, 1989: p. 15). A similar dilemma is faced by the writer of a newspaper article describing the difficulties faced by today's students. Although the writer begins his piece using *he* or *she*, after the first sentence he uses *he* as a generic pronoun:

> ... the student has to solve the same sort of problems as others of his age but, in so far as these may disturb his peace of mind and distract him, they can temporarily destroy his capacity to work. ... Thus, severe parental troubles, difficulties with the opposite sex, fear that his girlfriend may be pregnant ... can all bring effective work to a standstill
> (*Guardian*, 25 September 1992)

If *he* were truly a generic pronoun, the writer would have felt comfortable writing 'fear that *he* may be pregnant'. Clearly, this was rejected for sounding absurd – precisely because the use of *he* leads the reader to envision a male, not a male or female, student.

Such contradictions can lead to misunderstandings – when a writer uses *he*, how do we know when it is meant to be a 'generic' and when it is meant to apply to males only? It also, increasingly, puts readers off. Constantly referring to *he* and *his* when a writer is trying to reach a broad, mixed-sex audience will inevitably be interpreted as excluding women. Even if only some of your audience interprets it this way, you will be diminishing your impact.

Recommended solutions

There are several ways of avoiding the use of *he/him/his* when referring to men and women. The most common and easiest are listed below. Some solutions will work better in some situations than others; and in some cases, the meaning or tone may be slightly different. Sensitivity to context is important, as it is in all efforts to eliminate sexist language.

- Rewrite the sentence to avoid a pronoun. There are a few ways to do this. One is to use an article – 'a', 'an', 'the' – in place of the pronoun.

Example: 'A writer has his favourite handbook.'
Solutions: 'A writer has a favourite handbook.'
             'All writers have a favourite handbook.'
             'Writers have favourite handbooks.'

- Change the sentence to plural and use a plural pronoun.
             'Writers have their favourite handbooks.'

- Use both pronouns.
             'A writer has her or his favourite handbook.'
  (Note that this device should be used sparingly as it becomes cumbersome when the text contains many 'generic' pronouns.)

- Use a second-person pronoun ('you').
             'As a writer, you have your favourite handbook.'
  (Note that this solution changes the sense somewhat and can be considered too informal for some written documents. You might be more comfortable using this when speaking.)

- Use first-person plural ('we').
             'We writers have our favourite handbooks.'
  (Note that this solution also changes the sense somewhat.)

- Use 'one'.
             'As a writer, one has a favourite handbook.'
  (Again, this solution changes the sense somewhat by including the speaker/writer in the category of 'writers', which may not be what is intended. 'One' also carries class connotations for many readers.)

- Use 'the one'.

Example: 'He who laughs last, laughs longest.'

Solution: 'The one who laughs last, laughs longest.'

- Use a plural pronoun with a singular antecedent.

'Every writer has their favourite handbook.'

'Everyone has their favourite handbook.'

(Traditional grammarians will complain that this is incorrect usage. Yet it has a long history of respected users [Miller and Swift quote several famous writers who have used this technique, including George Bernard Shaw: 'It's enough to drive anyone out of their senses' (1989: 48).] It's also the way most of us speak now, when we find ourselves in a situation calling for the generic 'he'. It is more acceptable with antecedents such as 'everyone', 'anyone', 'one', and 'whoever'.)

- Alternate 'he' and 'she' within the text.

(This can be done by paragraph, section, or chapter. Be careful that its use does not reflect stereotyped assumptions about men and women and their roles – by, for example, using 'the doctor ... he' in one paragraph and 'the nurse ... she' in the next.

This technique has an added attraction in that people are not used to reading 'she' as a generic pronoun. Those who readily accept that 'he' means 'he or she' balk at the notion that 'she' can do the same thing. Using 'she' as a generic is a sure way to get such readers to reconsider what the use of 'he' conveys.)

- Use a compound of the two pronouns, such as 'he/she' or 's/he'.

'A writer has his/her favourite handbook.'

(This is most often objected to as awkward because it is not easy to read or speak and it stops the reader in midflow. It is useful in forms and contracts, however, when both options are offered with the intention that the inappropriate one will be crossed out.)

- Use 'that'.

Example: 'The rules confuse even the most sophisticated taxpayer, whoever he may be.'

Solution: 'The rules confuse even the most sophisticated taxpayer, whoever that may be.'

- Create or use a new, genderless pronoun.
  (This is of more academic than practical use. Although there is a long history of pronoun coinage, none of the suggestions has sufficiently caught on to be readily accepted by a reader. This is largely because they sound like alien language to us – 'hir', 'per', 'hesh', and 'co' are some of the suggestions. A nineteenth-century man in the United States proposed the word 'thon' (a contraction of 'that one') as a common-gender pronoun. Though logical, the term was never widely used, but it could be found in American dictionaries up until the 1950s (Miller and Swift, 1989, p. 60).

  Where familiarity is important, this is not the best option. Where creativity and some work by the reader play a part, it can be an interesting and useful alternative.)

There are other options for eliminating the 'generic' 'he/him/his', including replacing the pronoun with a noun or adjective.

Example: 'The student is expected to turn in his homework at the beginning of class.'

Solutions: 'The student is expected to turn in the previous night's homework at the beginning of class.'
             'The student is expected to turn in the assigned homework at the beginning of class.'

'It'

Another issue involving pronouns is the assignment of gender to inanimate objects. Referring to cars, ships and countries as 'she', for example, is sexist and is to be avoided. Use 'it' for inanimate objects, as well as for animals where the sex is unknown or unspecified.

* *

Q

quarryman OPTIONS: quarry manager, quarry worker.

quartermaster Because of its incorporation of the word MASTER, some consider this term sexist. In the US, it is a specific job title and has different meanings for different divisions of the military. OPTIONS: supplies officer, provisions officer, provisioner, commissary, storekeeper; navigator.

queen (noun) Use only in its literal sense for a female monarch, not as a general noun or modifier. Do not use it to refer to 'effeminate' homosexuals, although the term may be being reclaimed (turned into a positive label) within the homosexual community. See also KING; CHESS.
OPTIONS: ruler, monarch, sovereign, leader, figurehead, chief.

queen (adj) In some contexts, *queen* as a modifier has such a specific and well-understood meaning that to replace it might lead to misunderstandings (eg *queen bee*). If so, retain. Retain also for the mother of the ruling sovereign (*Queen Mother*) and when referring to the present monarch (eg *Queen's speech*, *Queen's counsel*). See also KING.
OPTIONS: royal, ruling, regal; top, leading, chief, paragon, ideal, most beautiful, the best, choice, prize.

queendom OPTIONS: empire, land, realm, region, territory, fief.

queen it (verb) OPTIONS: act superior, dominate (but see DOMINATE).

queenly OPTIONS: majestic, royal, regal, monarchical, noble, dignified, stately.

question master Because of its incorporation of the word MASTER, some people consider this sexist. See also QUIZMASTER.
OPTIONS: quiz show host (for female and male), questioner, quizzer, MC (see MASTER OF CEREMONIES), examiner.

quim Being reclaimed by women as a positive term for female genitals. See topic note on page 94.

quizmaster Because of its incorporation of the word MASTER, some people consider this sexist. See also QUESTION MASTER.
OPTIONS: quiz show host (for female and male), questioner, quizzer, MC (see MASTER OF CEREMONIES), examiner.

Quotations

There are several ways to deal with sexism in quotations. When quoting historical documents or figures, it is possible to paraphrase the quote and retain the original meaning. Replacing 'No man is an island' with 'No one is an island' conveys the same meaning and uses the same metaphor. If using the actual quotation is important, you could retain part of the quotation only, and complete the quotation with your own choice of words – no one 'is an island', for example; or you could omit the problematic word or words and replace with your own words in brackets – 'No [one] is an island', for example.

Historical quotations that contain sexist language can be used as examples to heighten people's awareness of how our sensitivities have changed since the quoted text was first read or spoken. Using *he* and *man* as 'generic' terms, intended to include women as well as men, is the most common problem that occurs. It may well be that when the statement was originally made or the document originally produced, it was widely accepted that *man* included *woman*. Now, however, to many ears this use of *man* jars.

One way to make use of sexism like this in quotations is to highlight the sexist word or words. Following the word with [sic] is a possibility, though it can be annoying to some readers. Another option is to highlight the word more subtly. This technique was used by a teacher who was faced every first day of the school year with presenting her students with a famous quote from Thomas Jefferson that read 'When the press is free, and every man able to read, all is safe'. She liked the quote and thought its message important enough to repeat to her students, yet hated perpetuating this sexist use of *man*. She wrote a small X under the word and, inevitably, by the second week of school her students figured out for themselves what the mark meant (Maggio, 1989).

You could, of course, simply leave the quotation as is, with no omissions or emphasis, on the understanding that your reader will place it in its historical context. When doing so, be sure that it will be placed in context, and that the sexist element will not be a distraction for you or your reader.

* *

R

rabbi Use for male and female.

radioman OPTIONS: radio technician, radio engineer, radio operator.

rag and bone man/ragman OPTIONS: rag picker, junk collector, junk dealer/vendor.

railwayman OPTIONS: railway worker; or be specific with, for example, conductor, porter, track layer, mechanic, engineer.

receptionist Use for male or female, and don't precede with 'male' if a man.

remittance-man Retain for historical accuracy. For general, inclusive use, replace with a more specific term.
OPTIONS: dependant, allowance receiver.

removal men OPTION: movers.

Renaissance man OPTIONS: Renaissance person, Renaissance woman/Renaissance man, person of many talents, well-rounded individual.

rent boy OPTIONS: prostitute, (sometimes) homosexual prostitute, (sometimes) gigolo.

repairman OPTIONS: repairer, service technician, fitter.

returner Often used in a sexist way to describe a woman who 'returns' to 'real' life (ie work, school) after spending years 'away' caring for children. It emphasises the presumption that the only worthy enterprise is that performed outside the home, and as such can be used to perpetuate discrimination against home-based workers (including homemakers). Would we refer to retired people as 'returners' when they leave the workplace? Be careful how the term is used.

rifleman OPTIONS: shooter, sharpshooter, gun handler, hunter, soldier.

right-hand man OPTIONS: right hand, assistant, aide, deputy.

ringmaster Because of its incorporation of the word MASTER, some people consider this sexist. See QUESTION MASTER.

OPTIONS: circus organiser/leader, circus host (for male or female), MC (see MASTER OF CEREMONIES).

Riot Grrl An effort (in this case by women in the contemporary music scene) to reclaim 'girl' as a positive label, with more assertive connotations (linking 'girl' with 'growl').

roundsman OPTIONS: deliverer, inspector, watch, patrol.

ruskmen See GINGERBREAD MEN.
OPTIONS: rusk figures, rusk people, ruskwomen and ruskmen.

rubbishman OPTIONS: rubbish collector, refuse collector.

S

sales girl/saleslady OPTIONS: salesperson, sales clerk, shop assistant, shopwalker, sales staff, sales representative, marketer, seller, cashier, till operator, saleswoman/salesman.

salesman OPTIONS: salesperson, sales clerk, shop assistant, shopwalker, sales staff, sales representative, marketer, seller, cashier, till operator, saleswoman/salesman.

schoolman OPTIONS: academician, scholar, lecturer, professor, academic.

schoolmarm See SCHOOLMARMY.
OPTIONS: schoolteacher, teacher, educator, instructor.

schoolmarmy Do not use as a general modifier; it perpetuates an outdated and sexist stereotype. Avoid, or replace with a more specific gender-neutral term that can be applied to men and women.
OPTIONS: old-fashioned, prim, prudish, tight-lipped, reserved.

schoolmaster/schoolmistress *Schoolmaster* is one of the few '–master' words that is used in a gender-specific way, so it is not in itself a sexist term. Nevertheless, its feminine 'counterpart', *schoolmistress*, suffers from the illicit and often derogatory connotations of MISTRESS as used today. Better to replace both with less loaded gender-neutral terms, as is increasingly being done in the educational community. See MASTER.
OPTIONS: head teacher, schoolteacher, teacher, educator, lecturer, instructor, principal.

scold (verb) Avoid using in a way that reinforces negative stereotypes of women. In such contexts, replace with a less loaded term that can be applied equally to women and men. See also BITCH; DOMINATE; NAG; PUSSY-WHIPPED; SHREW.
OPTIONS: gripe, reprimand, berate, chastise, bully, lecture, upbraid, lambaste, rail, abuse.

scold (noun) OPTIONS: pest, abuser, bully.

Scotsman This usage demonstrates that compounds with '–man' are not gender-neutral – consider the absurd sound of 'She's a Scotsman'. Replacing such terms can require reconstructing the sentence – such as by changing 'She's/He's a Scotsman' to 'She's/He's Scottish'. In this case, 'Scot' is also an acceptable alternative. For plural usage, 'the Scots' or 'the Scottish' is better than 'Scotsmen'. See topic note on page 63.

OPTIONS: a Scottish person, Scot, the Scottish, the Scots, person from Scotland.

Scouts No longer called Boy Scouts; one percent are girls. The association has changed some of its traditional rules: 'A Scout is a brother to all Scouts' has become 'A Scout belongs to the worldwide family of Scouts'. Similarly, 'A Scout has respect for himself and for others' has become 'A Scout has self-respect and respect for others' (*Independent*, 28 February 1994).

sculptress See topic note on page 26. OPTION: sculptor.

seaman OPTIONS: sailor, seagoer, seafarer, mariner, navigator.

seamanship OPTIONS: ship-handling expertise, navigation, navigation skill, sailing expertise, steerage, pilotry, sea legs.

seamstress Note the different connotations of *tailor*. See **topic note** on page 26.
OPTIONS: tailor, dressmaker, sewer, sewing machinist.

secretary Avoid the assumption that these are exclusively women; do not, for example, use 'male secretary'. This is an example of how stereotypes perpetuated by language can actually lead to discrimination: A recent poll of businesses found that 63 percent thought their workers would be amused to see a male secretary; 21 percent would be downright critical (*Independent*, 26 May 1993). Presumably, these companies would not hire a man for the job. One alternative would be to reserve *secretary* for Cabinet ministers and use *assistant* as a gender-neutral term free of derogatory connotations.

seductress This and similar terms (SIREN, TEMPTRESS) perpetuate an offensive stereotype of women. They blame women for men's behaviour, and excuse men by suggesting that they are not responsible for their sexual actions. If you must use, avoid the –ess ending and use *seducer* equally for men and women. See **topic note** on page 26.
OPTIONS: seducer, tempter, heartbreaker.

seminal Some object to this term's relation to 'seed/semen' as the source of creativity or value.
OPTIONS: original, germinal, originative, pivotal, influential, innovative. *Ovular* has been suggested as an alternative; see **topic note** on page 41.

serviceman/servicewoman 1. OPTIONS: service personnel (plural), member of armed services, recruit, officer, soldier, serviceman/servicewoman.

2. OPTIONS: servicer, technician, repairer, maintenance worker, mechanic.

shaman Not a sexist term; it derives from the Sanskrit for 'religious exercise' and is used for women and men.

Sharon A class-ridden and sexist term for a stereotyped woman who is considered tarty and tasteless, especially in dress. Has a masculine 'counterpart' in *Kevin*. See ESSEX MAN/GIRL.

she– Avoid preceding gender-neutral nouns (especially animal names) with 'she' to 'feminise' them, as in *she–wolf*.

shepherdess See topic note on page 26.
OPTION: shepherd.

sheila An Australian slang term for 'woman', as in 'sheila talk', or nattering. Avoid.

shipmaster Because of its incorporation of the word MASTER, some people consider this sexist.
OPTION: ship's captain.

shirtsleeves The phrase 'in one's shirtsleeves' assumes a male subject; women's shirts are usually called 'blouses'.
OPTIONS: jacket-less, casual, informal.

showgirl OPTIONS: dancer, chorus member, performer.

showmanship OPTIONS: dramatic flair, stagecraft, performance.

shrew An insult that reinforces negative stereotypes of women. Replace with a less loaded term that can be applied equally to women and men. See also BITCH; NAG; SCOLD.
OPTIONS: complainer, pest, grumbler, nuisance.

signalman OPTIONS: signal workers, signal operator, signaller.

single mother Better to use 'lone mother' (modelled on 'lone parent'); 'single' could be interpreted as 'unmarried', and marital status is not usually relevant when discussing the needs of parents (mothers or fathers) coping with children on their own. Even if you interpret 'single' to mean 'sole', 'single mother' has become a loaded term, nearly synonymous with 'parasite' and a target of Tory government campaigns. Better to replace.
OPTIONS: lone mother, lone parent, solo parent.

siren Perpetuates the stereotype of women as evil temptresses. Avoid.

sister 1. Retain for specific, female-sibling meaning or in religious contexts.
2. Replace when using as an adjective describing a close relationship – eg 'sister village', 'sister company'.
OPTIONS: neighbouring, twin, cousin, affiliated, associated, partner.
3. Replace in the health care context, as it has no parallel for men.
OPTIONS: charge nurse, head nurse, ward nurse, nurse.

sister company See SISTER.
OPTIONS: affiliated company, partner company.

sisterhood Use only for group of specifically female members. Unlike *brotherhood*, the term has also become associated with a solidarity movement among women; retain in this sense.
OPTIONS: unity, community, family, friendship, humanity, sibship, solidarity.

sister ship See SISTER.
OPTION: twin ship.

slag Offensive, and applied only to women in the sense of SLUT or WHORE (other meanings of *slag* are not sexist). There are no masculine equivalents with the same insulting connotations. See **topic note** on page 94.

sleeping policeman OPTIONS: speed bump, traffic bump.

slut Offensive, and loosely aplied to any woman who is considered to be sexually active and available. There is no masculine equivalent with the same insulting connotations, reflecting the double standard that it is unacceptable for women to be sexually promiscuous, but acceptable (even expected) for men to be. Avoid. See SLAG, WHORE, topic note on page 94.

snowman OPTIONS: snow creature, snow figure, snow sculpture, snowman/snowwoman (if specifically male or female), snow person.

sorceress See topic note on page 26.
OPTIONS: sorcerer, magician.

songstress See topic note on page 26.
OPTIONS: songster, singer, composer.

spaceman OPTIONS: astronaut, space explorer, cosmonaut.

spinster Some women are attempting to reclaim this as a positive term connected to its original meaning of 'one who spins'. It has many negative connotations not suffered by its masculine 'counterpart', BACHELOR, including 'old maid' and 'left on the shelf'. When marital status is relevant, replace. Otherwise, do not use unless using in its most literal sense of 'one who spins'.

OPTIONS: single, single person, single woman, unmarried person/woman.

spinster aunt An outdated concept. If marital status is relevant (which it usually is not), replace with 'unmarried aunt'. Otherwise, avoid. See also MAIDEN AUNT; OLD MAID; SPINSTER.

spokesman OPTIONS: spokesperson, leader, representative, speaker, PR coordinator, spokesman/spokeswoman. The *Independent* recommends using 'the company said' rather than 'a company spokesman said' (*Independent Style Book*, 1992); *The Times* prefers 'an official' (*The Times English Style and Usage Guide*, 1992).

sportsman OPTIONS: athlete, sports star, competitor, player.

sportsmanlike OPTIONS: fair, sporting, fair minded, square dealing.

sportsmanship OPTIONS: sporting ability, fair play.

squire Retain for historical accuracy; otherwise, avoid. See ESQUIRE.

stable lad/stable lass OPTIONS: stable hand, groomer.

stag party This and its counterpart *hen party* are both sexist in the associations made by their animal imagery. Men are often associated in positive ways with what are perceived to be strong, virile animals (*stag, stud*). Women, on the other hand, are associated 1) with the same animals but in a derogatory or contemptuous way (*nag, mare, ride*), and 2) with what are considered silly or frail animals (*hen, chick, filly*). See HEN PARTY.

OPTIONS: last-chance party, pre-wedding party.

starlet A derogatory term usually applied to minor-league female (but not male) actors who are assumed to have slept their way onto the screen.

OPTIONS: star, featured performer, minor star, inexperienced actor.

statesman OPTIONS: leader, politician, diplomat, ambassador.

statesmanlike OPTIONS: ambassadorial, diplomatic, tactful.

stationmaster/stationmistress *Stationmaster* is one of the few '–master' words that is used in a gender-specific way, so it is not in itself a sexist term. Nevertheless, its feminine 'counterpart', *stationmistress*, suffers from the derogatory connotations of '–mistress' as

used today. Better to replace both with less loaded gender-neutral terms. See MASTER; MISTRESS.
OPTIONS: station manager, station head.

steersman OPTIONS: pilot, steerer, navigator, guide, cox.

steward Not a sexist term; it derives from Old English for 'keeper of the hall'. It has come to be identified with men (as in STEWARD/STEWARDESS), though, so be careful how it is used.

steward/stewardess OPTIONS: flight attendant, flight crew member, cabin crew.

stockman OPTIONS: cattle breeder, sheep farmer, rancher.

straw man OPTIONS: straw figure, straw person, diversion, red herring.

strongman OPTIONS: weightlifter, iron pumper, powerhouse, tower of strength.

stuntman OPTIONS: stunt performer, daredevil, stuntwoman/stuntman.

suffragette The term began as a derogatory label for British women seeking the right to vote for women, but it was adopted by one section of the movement as a positive label, and continues to be used in that way. Other women (both in the UK and the US) preferred the term *suffragist*, which avoids the –ette suffix. See **topic note** on page 26.
OPTION: suffragist.

sugar daddy Avoid this term, which infantilises women and perpetuates harmful stereotypes. A feminine 'parallel', *sugar mama*, has been used – avoid this also.

suit As a slang term for 'business executive', *suit* has male connotations, though it could equally be used for women, who also wear suits. Unfortunately, it is not often used gender neutrally; a comparable term used for women is *shoulder-padded*.
OPTIONS: power broker, professional, executive, industrialist, high flier, corporate type.

swagman OPTIONS: vagrant worker, travelling labour, swagger, swaggie.

swordsman OPTIONS: sword fighter, swordsman/swordswoman, blade, fencer, sword, duellist.

swordsmanship OPTIONS: sword-handling skill, fencing ability.

Sex Words

There is a colourful array of slang terms for women that have
no parallel for men. Most are diminutives – 'sweet nothings'
that pretend to compliment women on their delicacy, softness,
sensitivity: some examples are *bird*, *babe*, *doll*. Many are
hateful, heaping scorn on women who have violated their
pedestal status or otherwise threatened men: *slut*, *slag* and
dog are among these. Jane Mills, in her book *Womanwords*,
presents a list of these 'defining women' words, terms that
have been used to describe women as anything other than
women: *beaver*, *hen*, *cow*, *bunny* (women as animals); *crumpet*, *tart*, *meat* (women as food); *skirt*, *bluestocking* (women
as clothing). More openly misogynistic are such terms as *cunt*,
tail, *leg* and *ass* (women as body parts).

Women's concerns about offensive language in the media
unfortunately have been linked to concerns about obscenity.
This perceived prudishness is a misconception: women are no
more upset by 'dirty' language and imagery than are men, and
it is not a feminist stance to object to nudity, explicit sex, or
swearing in themselves. What is objectionable, and what may
be being misinterpreted, is the predominant imagery of women
as sexual beings who are available for men's pleasure only.

The language of prostitution is an example of how sex
words are heavily weighted against women. There is a huge
vocabulary of demeaning slang terms for a female prostitute:
whore, *harlot*, *slut*, *tart*, *call girl*, *tramp*, *slag*, *slattern*. There
are many fewer for a male prostitute: *rent boy*, *gigolo*. For
men who pay prostitutes for sex, the slang terms are not
demeaning at all: *john*, *trick*, *punter*. This is part of the imbal-
ance of labelling the woman involved in an adulterous or
illicit relationship (*mistress*, *Lolita*, *bit of fluff*, *concubine*),
but not the man.

In terms of language used by women to describe their
bodies, there are few terms that are not or have not become
insults. Katharine Viner reported in the *Guardian* (9 July

1992) on the scarcity of words available to women for describing their genitals. She writes, 'Ask a man what he calls his penis and he will say his willy, prick, cock or Freddy. But ask a woman what she calls her genitals and she will reply with a coy, "Well, um, I don't really call them anything".' The words that are available are in general unsatisfactory: *fanny* is too soft and euphemistic (and carries the risk of misinterpretation; in the US, a fanny is a backside, male or female); *vagina* and *vulva* sound too clinical to many women.

Reclaiming insulting and derogatory terms may be one solution, and it certainly offers a wealth of choices: *pussy, cunt, quim.* (Some words that have enjoyed a moderate degree of success in being reclaimed include *spinster, bitch, babe, hag* and *crone.*) One problem with this is that a term's reclaimed, positive meaning is not always adopted by the entire community, so the effort is only partly successful. 'The fact remains that when the c-word is used as abuse, the intention behind it is violent and contemptuous' (Viner, *Guardian*, 9 July 1992).

Another option is to coin new terms. Participants in a writing workshop were given this task; they came up with *coombe*, a term used in Devon to refer to 'deep-sided valley', and *yoni*, a Sanskrit word meaning 'sacred representation of female genitals' (McNeill, 1992: 76).

For language to refer to sexual intercourse, it helps to use specific terms that describe the act, rather than euphemisms like 'make love'. Viner writes:

Terms used for the sexual act (in itself a misleading term, suggesting that there is just one 'sexual act') are all either mutual and gender-neutral – 'make love', 'have sex', 'do it', 'have it off' – or male-active – 'fuck', 'screw', 'penetrate', 'rod'. There is no female-active verb along these lines and I am pretty confident that my suggestions of 'envelop', 'engulf' and 'accommodate' won't sow the seeds of a lexical revolution.
(*Guardian*, 9 July 1992)

* *

T

talloress See SEAMSTRESS; topic note on page 26.
OPTIONS: tailor, sewer, dressmaker, sewing machinist.

talisman Not a sexist term; it derives from the Greek for 'consecrated object', and its plural form is *talismans*.

tart Now a derogatory term for a woman considered to be promiscuous, this term originally was an endearment, related to 'sweetheart'. Now it perpetuates the harmful notion that women dress provocatively (as prostitutes are thought to) to lure and entrap men. Avoid. See also topic note on page 94.

taskmaster/taskmistress See MASTER; MISTRESS.
OPTIONS: supervisor, boss, manager, overseer, inspector, controller, task sergeant, disciplinarian.

tasty That this term, most often used to describe a sexually attractive woman, is sometimes applied to men makes it no less sexist. Women are frequently being described in food terms ('tasty dish', 'crumpet'); when they are applied to men there is a tongue-in-cheek aspect that makes it less offensive. Women are also frequently described in terms of their appearance, so the alternatives are still unsatisfactory. See topic note on page 94.
OPTIONS: attractive, sexy, beautiful, handsome.

taxman OPTIONS: tax inspector, tax collector, Revenue/Inland Revenue staff; for general use, as in 'avoiding the taxman', use Inland Revenue.

tea lady OPTION: tea server.

temp Short for 'temporary employee', this applies to men as well as women, though the majority of temps are women and, no coincidence, highly exploited members of the workforce.

temptress This and similar terms (SIREN, SEDUCTRESS) perpetuate an offensive stereotype of women. They blame women for men's behaviour, and excuse men by suggesting that they are not responsible for their sexual actions. If you must use, avoid the –ess ending and use equally for men and women.
OPTIONS: tempter, seducer.

testimony Although it is etymologically related to *testicles* and *testos-*

terone, this term (like *contest* and *protest*) is not sexist. It derives from the Latin *testis* for 'witness'. Nevertheless, some object to its use; *ovarimony* has been coined as a woman-based alternative. See topic note on page 41.

thinking man OPTIONS: thinker, intellectual, philosopher, intelligent person, thinking woman/thinking man.

tigress See topic note on page 26.
1. For the animal, if distinguishing the sex is important, use 'female tiger'.
OPTION: tiger.
2. Offensive when used to describe a sexually available or aggressive woman. Avoid.

to a man OPTIONS: unanimously, everyone, of/with one voice, without exception.

toastmaster See MASTER.
OPTIONS: introducer, host, announcer, speaker, MC (see MASTER OF CEREMONIES).

to each his own See topic note on page 79.
OPTIONS: to each one's own, to each their own.

Tom, Dick, and Harry (every, any) OPTIONS: any ordinary person, every Tom, Jane, and Mary.

tomboy Characteristics which this is meant to describe – high spirited, physically active, daring – are not solely the domain of boys, so girls displaying them should not be compared to boys. Replace with a more specific term.
OPTIONS: athletic, sporty, high spirited, physically courageous, daredevil, active child.

tomcat If sex is relevant and not clear from the context, use 'male cat'. Otherwise, use 'cat'.

Tommy Retain for historical accuracy (from 'Tommy Atkins', the name used on model army forms in the nineteenth century). Otherwise, when referring to a contemporary British soldier, replace.
OPTIONS: private, soldier, recruit.

tommy gun Not a sexist term; this is actually a trademark and should technically be capitalised. It derives from John T Thompson, inventor of the Thompson sub-machine gun.

toyboy The masculine 'equivalent' of *bimbo* (only when used to refer to someone whose celebrated assets are physical rather than intellectual – *bimbo* is used more widely now than *toyboy*), this is objectionable for the same reasons – it perpetuates a sexist stereotype. Avoid.

townsman OPTIONS: resident, citizen, local, native, neighbour, member of the community, townsman/townswoman; (plural) townspeople, townsfolk.

tradesman 1. The best replacement for this is a more specific term. OPTIONS: technician, sub-contractor, builder, plumber, plasterer, decorator, construction worker, skilled worker, labourer.
2. OPTIONS: merchant, trader, shopkeeper, dealer; (plural) tradespeople, tradesfolk.

tradesmen's entrance OPTIONS: service entrance, traders' entrance.

tragedienne See topic note on page 26.
OPTION: tragedian.

trainman OPTIONS: railroader, train buff; conductor, driver, railroad worker, track layer.

trawlerman OPTION: trawler.

tribesman OPTION: tribe member.

triggerman OPTIONS: shooter, gangster, hired gun, sniper, sharpshooter, assassin.

tsar/tsarina Retain as sex-specific terms for Russian royalty. In a general context (meaning 'leader' or 'lord', as in 'drug tsar'), use *tsar* for women and men.

tutoress See topic note on page 26.
OPTION: tutor.

* * * * * * * * * * * **TOPIC NOTE** * * * * * * * * * * * *

Teachers and Teaching

The National Union of Teachers (NUT), National Association of Teachers in Further and Higher Education (NATFHE), and the Association of University Teachers (AUT) are three major teachers' organisations that have produced guidelines specifically covering non-sexist language. Below are some of the main points of these guidelines.

The NUT guidelines for equal opportunities in job recruitment mention just one aspect of language use, calling for the use of both feminine and masculine pronouns in job advertisements (it specifically mentions *s/he* and *her/him*) (*Fair and Equal*, 1991). A sample person specification in the guidelines avoids the problem by simply using the second person, *you*.

The NUT's *Towards Equality for Girls and Boys: Guidelines on Countering Sexism in Schools* has a section on language, which it says can be sexist in three main ways: 'by stereotyping females and males, by excluding women and girls, and by classing women and girls as inferior'. 'If stereotyped language is constantly used,' the document warns, 'pupils not only quickly pick up messages about suitable behaviour for their sex, but also appropriate future roles. For example, girls may be impeded from seeing themselves in those jobs or professions referred to only in the masculine form'. It mentions research findings showing 'that young children and even young adults consistently understand words including "man" such as "chairman" or "caveman" as masculine nouns and don't see women included in the meaning'. It also cites the adding of 'feminine' endings to words, saying 'this defines females as non-males, giving the impression the world is male unless proved otherwise'. The document states that avoiding such language 'is more accurate and often it is clearer and briefer.' Among the suggested actions to take is agreeing non-sexist guidelines to be included in the overall school policy.

Towards Equality, written by the NUT assistant secretary for equal opportunities and produced by ETUCE, a Europewide federation of teachers' unions (*Towards Equality*, ETUCE, 1992), urges every educational organisation to develop a policy on equal opportunities, beginning with a statement of intent covering all aspects of the curriculum, including 'measures to combat sex stereotyping including the provision of non-sexist books and teaching materials, [and] the use of non-sexist language and images'.

NATFHE's *An Equal Opportunities Guide to Language* (1993) is intended 'to produce a climate that allows discussion of change without people being in fear of using incorrect or unacceptable language; but also a climate in which sensitivity to the power of language is used as a positive force for developing genuine equality in the work place'. It defines non-sexist language as that which 'treats all people equally, and either does not refer to a person's sex at all when it is irrelevant, or refers to men and women in symmetrical ways when their gender is relevant'. It views the main problem of sexist language as that 'it assumes that the male is the norm. The words man, he, him are often used in referring to human beings of either sex. This gives a distinct impression to the reader or hearer that women are absent, silent, or of no importance.'

The Association of University Teachers (AUT) produced guidelines in 1984 (revised in 1991) covering non-sexist language. Among the suggestions are the use of *convenor* instead of *chairman*. A resolution to do away with the use of *he/his/him* and *man* and related compounds as generic terms has been implemented in the union's documentation and in oral communications. The AUT finds that using sexist language 'is not only confusing but also serves to perpetuate women's feelings of alienation from union activities, and results in their continued non-participation' (Deed, 1990). It also states that language 'which perpetuates, however unconsciously, inequalities in society or employment or stereotypical ideas of work roles is not conducive to the effective conduct of university business or to the achievement of equality of opportunity in university employment' (AUT, 1991).

* *

U

Ulsterman This usage demonstrates that compounds with ' –man' are not gender-neutral – consider the absurd sound of 'She's an Ulsterman'. Replacing such terms can require reconstructing the sentence – such as by changing 'She's/He's an Ulsterman' to 'She's/He's from Ulster'. You could also try 'Ulsterer'. See **topic note** on page 63.
OPTIONS: from Ulster, Ulster native, Ulsterer, Ulsterwoman/Ulsterman; (plural) Ulsterers, Ulsterfolk.

undergraduette An archaic example, devised in the 1930s, of the absurdity of feminising otherwise perfectly acceptable, gender-neutral terms.
OPTION: undergraduate.

undermanned OPTION: understaffed.

union man OPTIONS: union member, unionist, organised worker.

unman 1. OPTIONS: disarm, disempower, incapacitate, muzzle, silence, paralyse, handcuff, weaken, undermine.
2. OPTION: castrate (use in its literal sense only).

unmanly Not everyone associates the same characteristics with being *unmanly*. Better to replace with a more specific term that can be applied to men and women.
OPTIONS: cowardly, weak, timid, dishonest, dishonourable, cheap, small, rude.

unmanned OPTIONS: unstaffed, uncrewed, crewless, unpiloted, automatic, control-operated; uninhabited, empty.

unwed mother Do not use *mother* when you mean 'parents'. Usually, marital status is irrelevant; if it is relevant, use 'unmarried'. See SINGLE MOTHER.
OPTIONS: lone mother, lone parent; unmarried parents.

usherette See **topic note** on page 26.
OPTION: usher.

uxoricide There is no parallel term in use for 'killing one's husband' (*mariticide*, although technically 'husband–murder' – *maritus* is Latin for 'husband' – is rarely used and does not appear in most dictionaries). Interestingly, men who kill their wives, claiming to have been provoked by nagging or infidelity, have received negligible sentences or probation from British judges. Women who kill their husbands after years of violent abuse, in contrast, have in several cases been given long prison sentences, usually life.

uxorious There is no parallel term for submissively or excessively loving one's husband. The closest 'equivalent' is *wifely*, which (except when used ironically) is intended to carry the 'positive' connotation of a woman doing what is expected of a wife. *Uxorious*, on the other hand, carries entirely negative connotations.

V

valet Originally meant 'young man', and today usually refers to a male attendant.
OPTIONS: personal attendant, steward.

valet parking OPTION: parking service.

Valkyrie Retain when referring to women of Norse myth. Otherwise, avoid; it is sometimes used as a derogatory term for a woman considered strong, strident, or aggressive. See AMAZON.

vamp Replace with a gender-neutral term.
OPTION: seducer.

vampire Use for women and men.

VATman OPTIONS: Inland Revenue, tax collector, tax official, the Treasury, (sometimes) the Chancellor of the Exchequer.

vestryman OPTIONS: vestry member, parish councillor.

vicar Use for women and men.

vice-chairman See topic note on page 63.
OPTIONS: vice-chair, vice-chairperson, deputy, deputy director, vice-chairwoman/vice-chairman.

vice girl Avoid. For one thing, the person being referred to is usually a woman. If the person referred to provides sexual services for money, use PROSTITUTE. See topic note on page 94.

viceroy Derives from *roy*, French for 'king' and is a gender-specific title (the feminine 'equivalent' is *vicereine*). Retain for historical accuracy; otherwise, replace with a gender-neutral term.
OPTIONS: governor, vice-consul, deputy, regional governor.

vigilante Use for women and men.

vigilance man OPTIONS: vigilante, watch, guard.

villainess See topic note on page 26.
OPTION: villain.

virago Derives from *vir*, Latin for 'man', and is used derogatorily to refer to a woman considered noisy, loud, violent or domineering – in effect, a 'manly' woman. Being reclaimed by some feminists as a positive label (as in the feminist publisher Virago), but still used as an insult (as are *termagant*, *battleaxe*, *harridan*, XANTHIPPE and others). Use carefully. See also VIRTUE.

virgin (noun) Use this in a balanced way for women and men who have not yet had sexual intercourse.

virgin (adj) Because of its sexist connotations, some people object to using this term in the general sense of 'new' or 'unspoiled'. See also VIRGIN BIRTH.
OPTIONS: unspoiled, untouched, untainted, pristine, undeveloped, unprocessed, pure.

virginal Do not use as a general modifier meaning 'pure'. OPTIONS: pure, innocent, clean, white.

virgin birth A ridiculous term recently applied to women who have given birth without having had sexual intercourse. Their 'virginity' is irrelevant. If you mean 'artificial insemination' use that term. 'Parthenogenesis' is reproduction without being fertilised with male sperm; it only occurs among plants and, some believe, in the birth of Jesus.
OPTION: artificial insemination.

virile Use in a sex-specific context only in the sense of 'masculine'. Be careful how it is used. Otherwise, replace with a gender-neutral term.
OPTIONS: strong, vigorous, potent, powerful, dynamic, forceful.

virtue Derives from *vir*, Latin for 'man', and was probably originally used in the sense of 'courage'. At some point it also became associated with 'chastity' and was used for women only ('a woman of easy virtue'; avoid this usage.) It has come to be used as a gender-neutral term. See VIRAGO.

vixen Derives from 'female fox', and used as a derogatory term to describe a woman considered quarrelsome or spiteful. Avoid.

votaress OPTION: votary.

W

waitress See topic note on page 26.
OPTIONS: waiter, waitperson, server, serving staff, waitron.

waitress service OPTIONS: table service, waiter service, sit-down service.

Walkman Technically a trade name and so should not be used as a generic term.
OPTIONS: personal stereo, portable tape player, cassette player.

wardress See topic note on page 26.
OPTIONS: warder, warden, keeper, guardian.

warlock Originally meant 'traitor' or 'deceiver', and now can be used in the sense of 'evil sorcerer' of either sex.

warrior Use for men and women.

watchman OPTIONS: watch, guard.

weathergirl OPTIONS: weather forecaster, weather reporter, meteorologist.

weatherman OPTIONS: weather forecaster, weather reporter, meteorologist.

Weathermen The name of the terrorist group is Weathermen, though Weatherpeople and Weather Underground are also used.

Welshman This usage demonstrates that compounds with '–man' are not gender-neutral – consider the absurd sound of 'She's a Welshman'. Replacing such terms can require reconstructing the sentence – such as by changing 'She's/He's a Welshman' to 'She's/He's Welsh'. For plural usage, use 'the Welsh'. See topic note on page 63.
OPTIONS: Welsh, from Wales, native of Wales, Welshwoman/Welshman; (plural) the Welsh.

Wendy house Derives from the name of a fictional female character (Wendy in J M Barrie's *Peter Pan*), so it could be retained for historical/literary accuracy. But its widespread use in nurseries and playgroups could be off-putting to boys and could thus reinforce sexist stereotypes in play activities.
OPTION: play house.

werewolf Derives from 'man-wolf' and applies only to men; there is no feminine 'equivalent'.

whore Offensive, and applied only to women. There is no male equivalent with the same cheap and dirty connotations. Replace. See topic note on page 94.
OPTION: prostitute (for male or female).

whorehouse OPTIONS: brothel, paid-sex establishment, house of prostitution.

wide boy OPTIONS: unscrupulous trader, rip-off artist, dodgy dealer.

widow/widower An unusual case in which the feminine form is the standard and the masculine form is the derivative. *Widower* was only coined in the fourteenth century, probably because for a long time only women were considered to have been left stranded and identity-less upon the death of their spouse, thus needing a label for their changed circumstances.
OPTION: widow (for female and male).

wife/wives Be careful how these are used. 'The neighbour's wife', for example, is actually a neighbour herself. Also, referring to a certain group 'and their wives' is not only offensive but inaccurate. 'MPs' wives' are only some of the spouses who benefit from paid overseas travel; MPs' husbands do also. To speak of 'the wives of US servicemen' refers to only some of the Army spouses, and would be better worded 'the spouses of US service personnel (or members)'.
OPTIONS: spouse, partner, mate, wives and husbands.

wimmin A word coined by feminists to replace 'women', which by incorporating the word 'men' can give the appearance of sexism, although it is not etymologically a sexist term. Has been adopted by some feminist publications. See WOMAN; topic note on page 41.

wireman OPTION: electrician.

wise man OPTIONS: sage, expert, adviser, decision-maker, judge, consultant. A 'panel of wise men' could be 'a panel of experts'.

witch Use for women and men. The masculine 'equivalent', *wizard*, has different connotations.

woman (noun) Not a sexist term; it derives from *wifman*, Old English for 'female human being'.

woman (adj) Do not use as a modifier (as in 'woman police officer'). If the gender of the person is relevant (which it often is not) and is not implied by the context, restructure the sentence: 'A police officer was killed today. She was the ninth. . .' or 'The force was made up of 15 female officers and 25 male officers'. When you are tempted to use 'woman' as a modifier, test yourself: would you also use 'man' in the same way? If not, do not use 'woman'.

–woman Compound words with '–woman' (*spokeswoman*, *saleswoman*) can sometimes be used, in a sex-specific sense, where '–man' compounds would also be used. Some have a long history as parallel terms: *gentlewoman*, for instance – *gentleman* has never been used as a generic term encompassing women and men. For plural usage, it is often possible to use both terms – *craftsmen and craftswomen*, for instance – but in most cases it is preferable to use a gender-neutral alternative. See topic note on page 63.

womaniser There is no parallel term for women; the closest terms for women all carry insulting, less glamorised connotations – SLUT, WHORE, and the more active MAN-EATER. Replace with a gender-neutral term. See PHILANDERER.
OPTION: philanderer.

womanish An insulting term used to describe someone or something considered weak, fickle, frail, or ineffective – so-called feminine qualities. Avoid. See FEMININE.

woman's intuition OPTIONS: intuition, hunch, sixth sense.

women and children Heard often to describe the 'innocent victims' of war (as in 'women and children first'); offensive to both women and men. If necessary, distinguish between civilians and soldiers. Otherwise, avoid making arbitrary distinctions between kinds of victim.

women's libber A derogatory term for a feminist. See FEMINIST.
OPTIONS: feminist, women's rights campaigner, equal rights supporter/campaigner.

working mother Implies that not all mothers are working, and reflects capitalist society's attitude towards non-wage-based activities. Use 'working outside the home' or specify profession/job if necessary.

working woman See CAREER WOMAN.
OPTION: worker.

workmanlike OPTIONS: skilful, competent, efficient.

workmanship OPTIONS: craft, skill, artisanry, expertise; or be specific with, for example, carpentry, woodworking, carving.

workman OPTIONS: builder, contractor, labourer, worker.

workman's cottage OPTION: worker's cottage.

WPC The 'W' prefix (as in WPC: woman police constable) before rank is unique to the police and is on its way out. Drop the 'W'; if gender is relevant (which it often is not), make it clear from the context by using the first name, a feminine pronoun or restructuring the sentence to include 'who is a woman'. See WOMAN (adj); topic note on page 76.
OPTIONS: PC, constable, police officer.

Wren The women's division of the Royal Navy (WRNS), from which this term derives, no longer exists; women are now part of the Royal Navy. Although it is still used within the Royal Navy (for example, in certain job titles – 'Wren cook') to distinguish female from male personnel, it is not necessary and should be avoided. Although some former Wrens may be proud of the title, many other Navy women may see it as a way to trivialise their role.

X

Xanthippe Use only in reference to the historical figure, not as a general term describing a woman considered to be quarrelsome or shrewish. Replace with a more specific term that can be applied to men and women, but avoid using these in a way that reinforces negative stereotypes of women. See also NAG; PUSSY-WHIPPED; SCOLD.
OPTIONS: quarrelsome person, pest, irritant.

Y

yachtsman OPTIONS: yacht owner, yacht racer, sailor, yachtsman/yachtswoman.

Yankee Derives from *Jan*, a nickname for Dutchman, but is used inclusively for women and men.

yeoman 1. OPTIONS: freeholding farmer; attendant, helper.
2. Retain in official title of Yeoman of the Guard.
For general use, replace with a gender-neutral term.
OPTIONS: beefeater; warder, bodyguard.
Retain in official title of signaller in Royal Navy or Marines.

yeomanly OPTIONS: loyal, brave, courageous, stalwart, staunch.

yes man OPTIONS: follower, sycophant, supporter, assenter, servant.

yesterday's man OPTIONS: faded politician, yesterday's woman/yesterday's man.

yob/yobbo Like *youth*, these are often used specifically for young men (*yob* possibly derives from back slang for 'boy' from the nineteenth century), but can be used for young women as well. See YOUTH.

yogini The feminine 'equivalent' of *yogi*.
OPTION: yogi.

Yorkshireman This usage demonstrates that compounds with '–man' are not gender-neutral – consider the absurd sound of 'She's a Yorkshireman'. Replacing such terms can require reconstructing the sentence – such as by changing 'She's/He's a Yorkshireman' to 'She's/He's from Yorkshire'. See topic note on page 63.

OPTIONS: from Yorkshire, native of Yorkshire, Yorkshirewoman/Yorkshireman.

youth/youths Often used to mean 'young men', but is not gender specific and in some contexts can be used for both women and men (as in the 'youth of today'). Be aware that it is often interpreted as masculine; you might want to replace with a gender-neutral alternative. OPTIONS: teenager, adolescent, minor, youngster, kid, juvenile.

Bibliography

Ayto, John, *Dictionary of Word Origins* (Bloomsbury, London, 1990).

Ayto, John and Simpson, John, *The Oxford Dictionary of Modern Slang* (Oxford University Press, Oxford, 1992).

Baron, Dennis, *Grammar and Gender* (Yale University Press, New Haven/London, 1986).

Cameron, Deborah, *Feminism & Linguistic Theory* (Macmillan, London, 1985).

Darter, Pat, 'English as She is Written', *Terminologie et Traduction* 2/89, European Communities: Office of Official Publications.

Deed, Robyn, 'Comment: A Non-sexist Guide', *Fawcett News* 1990.

Frank, Francine Wattman and Treichler, Paula A, *Language, Gender, and Professional Writing: Theoretical Approaches and Guidelines for Nonsexist Usage* (The Modern Language Association of America, New York, 1989).

Gowers, Sir Ernest, *The Complete Plain Words* (Penguin Books, London, 1987).

Green, Jonathon, *New Words: Dictionary of Neologisms Since 1960* (Bloomsbury, London, 1991).

Howard, Philip, *A Word in Time* (Sinclair-Stevenson, London, 1990).

Kramarae, Cheris and Treichler, Paula A, *Amazons, Bluestockings and Crones: A Feminist Dictionary* (Pandora, London, 1992).

Lederer, Richard, *The Miracle of Language* (Pocket Books, New York, 1991).

McNeill, Pearlie, *Because You Want To Write: A Workbook for Women* (Scarlet Press, London, 1992).

Maggio, Rosalie, *The Nonsexist Word Finder: A Dictionary of Gender-free Usage* (Beacon Press, Boston, 1989).

—— *The Bias-Free Word Finder: A Dictionary of Nondiscriminatory Usage* (Beacon Press, Boston, 1991).

Miller, Casey and Swift, Kate, *The Handbook of Non-Sexist Writing* (The Women's Press, 2nd British edition, London, 1989).

Mills, Jane, *Womanwords* (Virago Press, London, 1991).

—— *Sexwords* (Penguin Books, London, 1993).

Nash, Walter, *Jargon: Its Uses and Abuses* (Blackwell, Oxford, 1993).

Partridge, Eric, *A Dictionary of Slang and Unconventional English* (Routledge & Kegan Paul, London, 1984).

Poynton, Cate, *Language and gender: making the difference* (Oxford University Press, Oxford, 1989).

Rees, Nigel, *The Politically Correct Phrasebook* (Bloomsbury, London, 1993).

Ricks, Christopher and Michaels, Leonard, eds. *The State of the Language* (Faber and Faber, London, 1990).

Spender, Dale, *Man-Made Language* (Routledge & Kegan Paul, London, 1985).

Wren, Brian, 'Language Change and Male Repentance', in *Who Needs Feminism?: Men Respond to Sexism in the Church*, ed. Richard Holloway (SPCK, London, 1991).

Specific Guidelines

Association of University Teachers (AUT), 'Non-Sexist Language' (circular distributed to local associations), April 1991.

British Psychological Society, 'Guidelines for the Use of Non-sexist Language', *The Psychologist*, February 1988.

British Sociological Association, 'BSA Guidelines of Anti-sexist Language', 1989.

The Independent Style Book 1992.

Making Women Visible: The Use of Inclusive Language Within the ASB. A Report by the Liturgical Commission of the General Synod of the Church of England (Church House Publishing, London, 1988).

National Organization for Women (NOW), 'Practical Guide to Non-Sexist Language', 1989.

National Union of Journalists, 'Equality Style Guide' (NUJ Equality Council, London, no date).

—— 'Images of Women: Guidelines for Promoting Equality through Journalism' (NUJ Equality Council, London, 1986).

National Union of Teachers, 'Fair and Equal: Union Guidelines for Promoting Equal Opportunities in the Appointment and Promotion of Teachers' (NUT, 1991).

—— 'Towards Equality for Girls and Boys. Guidelines on Countering Sexism in Schools' (NUT, no date).

National Union of Teachers of Further and Higher Education, 'An Equal Opportunities Guide to Language' (NATFHE, 1993).

The Times English Style and Usage Guide (Times Books, London, 1992).

'Towards Equality' (ETUCE, 1992).

The Women's Press is Britain's leading women's publishing house. Established in 1978, we publish high-quality fiction and non-fiction from outstanding women writers worldwide. Our exciting and diverse list includes literary fiction, detective novels, biography and autobiography, health, women's studies, handbooks, literary criticism, psychology and self help, the arts, our popular Livewire Books for Teenagers young adult series and the bestselling annual *Women Artists Diary* featuring beautiful colour and black-and-white illustrations from the best in contemporary women's art.

If you would like more information about our books, please send an A5 sae for our latest catalogue and complete list to:

The Sales Department
The Women's Press Ltd
34 Great Sutton Street
London EC1V 0DX
Tel: 0171 251 3007
Fax: 0171 608 1938

Also of interest:

The Women's Press Handbook Series

Casey Miller and Kate Swift
**The Handbook of Non-Sexist Writing
for Writers, Editors and Speakers**

Third British Edition – Fully revised and updated

How can we avoid sexist language and find clear and
elegant ways of saying what we mean? In this
definitive handbook, Casey Miller and Kate Swift
offer essential solutions to the use of sexist clichés,
suffixes, prefixes, pronouns, titles, categories and
terms. Now fully revised and updated, here is a lively
and informative companion for any writer, journalist,
teacher, editor and lover of the English language.

'An essential aid for anyone who makes his or her
living out of words, as well as a sensible guide for
people who know that an even-handed language
would help towards an even-handed world.'
Cosmopolitan

Reference/Language/Women's Studies £6.99
ISBN 0 7043 4442 4

Susan Sellers, editor
Taking Reality by Surprise
Writing for Pleasure and Publication

With Michèle Roberts, Zoë Fairbairns, Joan Riley,
Caeia March, Amryl Johnson, and many, many more...

Over fifty editors, literary agents and writing tutors,
as well as novelists, journalists, poets and playwrights
– all leaders in their field – offer a complete guide to
writing and getting published for accomplished and
aspiring writers alike.

From starting out to choosing the appropriate genre,
from finding the right outlet to keeping the momentum
going, here is a wealth of advice, hands-on exercises
and useful contacts.

'Gets enthusiasts past the " I've always wanted to
write but..." stage. Excellent.' *Daily Telegraph*

Creative Writing £8.99
ISBN 0 7043 4267 7

Conjured by Mary Daly
in cahoots with Jane Caputi
**Websters' First New INTERGALACTIC
WICKEDARY of the English Language**

'Mary Daly's own mind is a-buzz with puns and
inventions of considerable wit and ingenuity...
Mary Daly is a "fumerist" of the first league.'
Times Educational Supplement

Fumerist: A feminist humorist who makes sparky
incendiary blazes of light...who makes whys cracks.

**Websters' First New Intergalactic Wickedary of the
English Language:** An illustrated guide to the
creating, spelling and new meanings of words. Mary
Daly sweeps out man-made language and, with
wicked inspiration, ushers in a vital, new and mind-
expanding vocabulary. The most joyous, irreverent
and hilarious 'alter-dictionary' ever to hit the shelves.

'Roistering, rambunctious, tickling and tumbling.'
New York Times

Reference £12.99
ISBN 0 7043 4114 X